WARREN BRYAN MARTIN

Alternative
To
Irrelevance

A STRATEGY FOR REFORM
IN HIGHER EDUCATION

ABINGDON PRESS
NASHVILLE & NEW YORK

ALTERNATIVE TO IRRELEVANCE

A version of Chap. III, under the title "The Will To Be Different," was originally published in *Saturday Review*, January 21, 1967, and is used here by permission. Chap. IV, "The Problem of Size," first appeared in the March, 1967, issue of *The Journal of Higher Education* (Ohio State University Press), and is reprinted by permission. Parts of Chap. V, under the title "Should Students Rule?" appeared in *Matrix '67*. Reprinted from *Matrix '67*, a service of *motive*, by permission. Portions of Chap. V, under the title "Student Participation in Academic Governance," appear in *In Search of Leaders*, the 1967 volume of *Current Issues in Higher Education*. It is used here by permission of the American Association for Higher Education. Parts of Chap. V, entitled "The University as Community," appear in the Fall, 1967, issue of *The Educational Record*; reprinted by permission of *The Educational Record* and its publisher, the American Council on Education. A version of Chap. VI, entitled "An Answer for Anomie," was printed in the *Teachers College Record*, vol. LXVIII, October, 1966, and appears here by permission.

SET UP, PRINTED, AND BOUND BY THE
PARTHENON PRESS, AT NASHVILLE,
TENNESSEE, UNITED STATES OF AMERICA

TO ELIZABETH

FOREWORD

Among students and those who work closely with them, the burning question today is whether reform of their universities or of the larger society can be brought about by activities "within the system."

The university's failings, both as an educational institution and as a meliorative force in society, have become the objects of reformist zeal. Increasing numbers of students, led by the brightest and most conscientious among them, want to reduce the discrepancies between the promise and the realities of the university's educational activities. The focus of attention may be upon a set of rules that seems to have been made without the needs of students in mind, a curriculum that seems too remote from the great issues or problems of the day, teaching that seems poorly motivated and ethically neutral, or an institutional management that seems willing to sacrifice justice, freedom, and truth in the interests of power and success. Can students who have become aroused by issues in these areas do anything to improve matters through democratic procedures, or must they, because of their own impatience or the immutability of the university system, choose between the personally demoralizing alternative of dropping out psychologically and the socially dangerous alternative of confrontation politics?

When students look to the national scene, they find little to give them hope or inspiration. They are as aware as anybody else of the crisis of our times—a crisis which has forced good men to ask whether our empire building, which is borne upon the most powerful technology ever conceived, can be brought into the service of humanity and democracy. Students are deeply involved in this crisis, if for no other reasons, because of the draft law. This law not only demands that they give themselves and perhaps their lives to dubious national policies—policies opposed by almost everybody they have reason to respect—but it throws the best of them into a soul-trying moral conflict: having won self-respect through participation—vicarious if not active—in the civil rights movement, they are now invited to save themselves by staying in college while the heaviest burden is carried by their less privileged brothers. Will the university, with its enormous power and its responsibilities for upholding the basic values of Western civilization, do anything about this, or must the whole matter be left to students and the individual supporters they can find?

Professor Martin assumes that reform must be brought about within the system. He addresses himself to educators, because he sees that it is only they who, in the face of mounting external pressures, can keep their institutions oriented toward humanistic goals. Controlling his moral fervor, he maintains a tone of reasonableness and suggests that reform may not be very difficult: it may be achieved through the establishment of alternative models for higher education, of which the cluster college is the most promising example. We shall see what happens. We shall see whether his sound and moderate proposals are too little and too late.

Professor Martin does not undertake in this volume the social analysis that would be necessary to show just how external pressures impinge on the university, and how that institution might cope with them, nor does he take up the even more difficult and critical question of how the university might influence the course of events on the national scene. One might hope that he will next bring his ethical sensitivity and analytical powers to bear on these problems.

Nevitt Sanford

PREFACE

The essays of this book are influenced by two assumptions. The first one is that learning in the twenty-first century will take place under arrangements so radically different from present educational forms that the ways we do things now are not likely to have much transfer value then. The second assumption is that the content of educational programs in the future will be changed no less radically than the forms; indeed, changed to such an extent that what we teach today may be regarded by educators in the next century as negative precedents—examples of what not to do.

Present, rapid transformations in post-industrial technology and the growing impact of new media are harbingers of the extent of changes coming in the forms of education, while the emerging challenges of the young to prevailing societal values—to war as an instrument of national policy, to the social and ethical hypocrisies of our culture, to power, fame, and wealth as life goals—are evidence that traditional values are no longer assumed to be good and, increasingly, are regarded as deficient. The forms and the substance of life in this nation are beginning to change in ways so profound that it seems imperative to recognize that the future of higher education is going to be different, not in degree, but in kind.

With revolutionary changes coming in our colleges and universities because of external influences that cannot be denied, the core problem today is to devise ways for educational institutions to open themselves to criticism and to creative alternatives without sacrificing that measure of independence necessary to save them from arbitrary or capricious change.

My response to this problem is in the form of two proposals. The first one asserts that an atmosphere of openness to substantial changes would be encouraged by the establishment of alternative models for higher education, models that would show a degree of structural variety and value diversity not found in existing institutional arrangements. The second proposal is that the recently formulated cluster college concept, whereby small colleges can be organized as centers of experimentation within large universities, is the best mechanism known to us now for testing divergent models. This concept encourages a university to develop educational prototypes, yet without altering its total organization; and, additionally, the concept offers a way to legitimize educational change-probes by bringing them under the aegis of established institutions.

These essays, then, are an act of advocacy. Informed by research data, but not limited to statements guaranteed by that data, they posit the need for radical change. Yet they urge that the best way to achieve it would be to employ, given the nature of university life, an essentially conservative strategy—one that does not call for the elimination of existing programs but rather for the creation of alternative futures, perhaps by the organization of cluster colleges. These, hopefully, would extend the range of acceptable styles and emphases in academe and, in a way consistent with the American tradition of pluralism and diversity, help us to see how limiting the old educational monolith has been and how notable must be the changes if we are to make higher education meaningful for new youth in new times.

Three of these essays were presented in slightly different form at the 20th Annual Institute of Higher Education, sponsored by the Division of Higher Education, Board of Education, The Methodist Church. Sections of the total manuscript have appeared in various publications, including the *Saturday Review*, the *Teachers College Record*, the *Journal of Higher Education*, the *Educational Record*, the *Research Reporter*, Center for Research and Development in Higher Education, University of California, Berkeley, *Matrix '67*, and *In Search of Leaders*, the 1967 volume of *Current Issues in Higher Education* (AAHE).

Harriet Renaud, Julie Pesonen, and Edyth Short made important editorial suggestions and emendations to the text. Lilly Grenz and Moffett Hall were typists of skill and good judgment. Research assistants David Kamen and Catherine Lyon, no less than the others, combined efficiency and humanity in the work for which they were responsible.

CONTENTS

13

CONTENTS

I

THE NEED FOR
ALTERNATIVE MODELS

Lewis Mumford's essay *The Transformations of Man* traces several cultural epochs through which man has passed in his development from animal toward unified self. Mumford first describes archaic man— earthbound, worshiping the gods of vegetation, in tune with the rhythm of the seasons, securing his future by holding tightly to the past.[1] Then came civilized man, whose society was characterized by social divisions and role specialization, externalized law and codified behavior, hierarchical authority and the institutionalization of energy. The third epoch belonged to axial man. He appeared about the sixth century B.C., at widely separate points, and can be identified with various religious movements that emerged about the same time.

[1] Mumford, *The Transformations of Man* (New York: Collier Books, 1956), p. 32.

The central change brought about by axial religion was the redefinition—in fact, the very recasting—of the human personality. Values that emerge only in the personality replaced those that customarily belonged to institutions.[2] Axial man purified his animal nature and emphasized, not primarily material values, but spiritual ones, and especially the value of the individual.

Archaic, civilized, and axial man, taken together, represent what Mumford calls the Old World. But all that is behind us now. Our world, the New World, came in with the Renaissance, prospered by reducing external limitations on human power and exalting human potential, and, under the impetus of rationalism, empiricism, and the scientific methodology, has come to be characterized by technological man. But each epoch had its hazards, and the danger now is that technique will become everything and man's humanness will be lost. That would mean the advent of post-historic man. "In the post-historic scheme," Mumford writes, "man becomes a machine, reduced as far as possible to a bundle of reflexes: rebuilt at the educational factory to conform to the needs of other machines." [3] The victory of this style of life, he says, will effectively do away with any serious reason for remaining alive.[4]

[2] *Ibid.*, p. 61.
[3] *Ibid.*, p. 125.
[4] *Ibid.*, p. 132.

It is the commitment to man truly alive—intellectually, spiritually, individually, collectively, at a time when evidence points to the advent of post-historic man—that gives credibility and urgency to the developing concern of national leaders for change and direction in higher education. They sense that if man is to become a unified self, nothing less than a comprehensive attack must be made on the problems that presently block this achievement. Many of these problems are in the social environment, but they cannot be overcome unless man as an individual is changed. Thus, as Mumford puts it:

Man's principal task today is to create a new self, adequate to command the forces that now operate so aimlessly and yet so compulsively. This self will necessarily take as its province the entire world, known and knowable, and will seek, not to impose a mechanical uniformity, but to bring about an organic unity, based upon the fullest utilization of all the varied resources that both nature and history have revealed to modern man. . . . In short, the moment for another great historic transformation has come.[5]

Indeed. But creating a new self for man will not be possible without changes in the social setting that are correspondingly radical. The behavioral sciences show that forces in the environment have a reciprocal influence on the change agent, man. What man is in-

[5] *Ibid.*, p. 134.

fluences what he does. Yet what he does, and where he does it, influences what he is.

The next historic transformation of man will require that the total environment, understood as the world culture, be utilized in man's education, even as all of his learning will need to be applied to the total environment. This is the magnitude of the challenge before us. And the immediate question is this: Can our present educational system, particularly higher education, contribute to such a transformation?

One to two percent of college-age youth answer "No." Their view is that an educational institution can provide, because of its nature, only institutional education—something as dull as institutional food but not even as nourishing. Colleges and universities are part of the social system, deriving support from agencies and individuals that tolerate only traditional values and approved arrangements. Institutional responses to contemporary challenges can be expected, therefore, to be predictably sound, all sound—"sound and fury, signifying nothing." Transformations of man will require revolutions in social organizations; but the schools have been bought off, brought to terms with the Establishment, and made part of a past that is dying. Most educators, of course, are unwilling to allow that education is in a state of crisis, but to these young people the crisis is past and what remains is not a healthy organism but more nearly a corpse. Their view is that present efforts at innovation are just flowers at the patient's bedside, that administrative pleas for communication between students and faculty are futile because the cancer in the body politic is terminal, that there is nothing more to be said save condolences. Administrators will restore quiet to the campus, but it will be the quiet of a graveyard.

Another minority element, but larger in numbers and with a broader representation, agrees that much of current educational practice has no life and should, therefore, be interred. Yet for these students and faculty the ancient Egyptian legend of the phoenix is an imperfect but instructive analogy. They believe that what has been consumed in fire by its own act can yet rise again in youthful freshness from its ashes. (The concept that the dead may live again has Christian as well as Egyptian precedent.) Institutional education—formal, impersonal, self-satisfied—is going under now, burning itself out as it goes and, in what it calls its successes, piling up only ashes. But those ashes can nourish the soil on which new beginnings may be built. The coterie of the concerned need not move to Bohemia; they can build profitably in Berkeley, Chicago, or New York. The new will be built, not on the old foundation but on the ground of earlier efforts. This is the way to secure nourishment from tradition without being bound to its forms.

This reform minority has appeal for many of us in

higher education. We are disheartened about the prospects for partial and piecemeal innovations and have come to believe that only radical reforms will qualify our colleges and universities for leadership in the next historic transformation of man. Yet we are not ready to join the smaller minority, the repudiation party, and forsake the institution. We may feel toward the school as Noah must have felt concerning his forty-day sojourn in the ark: "If it hadn't been for the storm outside, we couldn't have taken the smell inside." So it is with us. We stay with the ark. We are not ready to abandon ship, nor even to mutiny, but we are in a mood for radical reforms. However, it must be added that most of our colleagues seem content with things as they are, as evidenced by the fact that they oppose experimentation and are uneasy about even modest innovation.

How, then, can a start be made toward substantive change? The first step, I believe, should be the creation of viable alternative models for educational institutions. At present, despite pretensions to diversity, we have as the ideal for colleges and universities variations of only one model. That model is the "versity," and its variations are the miniversity, the university, and the multiversity. In the "versity," no matter what the size, institutional success is measured by the familiar emphases of today's academic guilds—organization by subject-matter departments and/or schools, curricula arranged accordingly, and faculty hired by specializations and promoted more on the basis of research and publications than of teaching competency.

Almost all liberal arts colleges, having no respectable, challenging alternative models for their future, are trying to become miniversities—first in the character and style of faculty and later, indeed as soon as possible, in the variety and complexity of programs. But a "versity" by any other name is still a "versity"; differences are only of degree. It is regrettable that, no matter now inappropriate the established model for particular colleges, nearly all strive for its rewards and adhere to its sanctions. Such conformity confirms the sagacity of Ben Franklin's remark that "people fear being out of style more than they fear hell."

As liberal arts colleges try to become miniversities, so state colleges set their sights on becoming universities; and now within the last decade universities aspire to join the multiversities. But here, too, the values of the "versity" dominate; indeed, they are more conspicuous than elsewhere. Universities and multiversities are professionally oriented with regard to faculties and, as for curricula, they are service centers for a technological society.

Our concerns regarding this pervasive model are not based on the claim that what it does is bad—society must be served, and those who train society's workers ought to be professionally competent. Rather, a pluralistic society must have diversity in models if we are to avoid tyranny or anarchy—diversity that we do not now have. Furthermore, our dominant model lacks the flexibility necessary to adapt to the radically different emphases required for the education of man in the nuclear-electronic age. The prime need now in higher education is for men and institutions who have the courage to investigate possibilities for alternative futures, to shape them into actual models, and to put those plans to the test of practice.

But how do we start such a process when so many faculty and administrators are content with what they have, preferring the known to the unknown for all the reasons explained by psychology and religion, and operating as they are without attractive options (the consequence of monocracy)? How are we to create an atmosphere that would make them receptive to divergent ideas, shake complacency or false assurances, and invite leadership for innovation and experimentation?

The best hope, it seems to me, for encouraging an interest in change is in showing the inherent conflicts in the dominant educational model and, at the same time, probing for alternative ideas and forms that might resolve these conflicts and provide better responses to the challenges emerging now.

What are the conflicts in the present situation, and what are some of the alternatives?

CONFLICTING PHILOSOPHICAL
ASSUMPTIONS

In the realm of educational philosophy there are conflicts caused by the professorial claim to certainty in some disciplines and the refusal in others to make values anything more than personal preferences.

Based on the confidence of the eighteenth and nineteenth centuries in an ordered and orderly universe, the viewpoint developed that an intellectual, working in his specialization and employing empirical data, can speak with clarity and objectivity, free of personal value biases. This claim to certainty is now seriously challenged by the natural sciences; the old assumption of a static universe has been replaced by that of a dynamic one. J. Robert Oppenheimer has described the change this way:

The unity of knowledge, long thought of as corresponding to a structure in which the foundation stones imply the whole, has today a very different topology; very much more than a temple, it is a network, as William James foresaw, with no central chamber, no basic truths from which all else will follow, but with a wonderful mutual relevance between its many branches, and with beauty illuminating the growing tips of knowledge, even in the most recondite and unfamiliar branches.[6]

[6] Oppenheimer, "The Added Cubit," *Encounter*, XXI (1963), 44-47.

Evidence of a universe of contingency and change has brought humility to natural scientists, but not to some professors in the social and behavioral sciences. Those of a positivist bent have been slower to admit either their finitude or the complexity and mystery of what they study, and it is possible still to encounter among them rather pompous claims to value-free instruction, scholarly objectivity, and other features of a so-called science of man.

It was David Hume who showed, in his own work, but contrary to his intentions, that a science of man is not possible. The very data on which such a science must rely, taken as they are from a wide range of human experiences, always remain problematic, selective, and in some measure reflective of the observer's preferences. Hume found that

one needed to know facts about the past to find out "the springs and principles" of the human mind; but one had, at the same time, to decide what these springs and principles were in order to reach a decision, and even then only a strictly personal decision, as to what the facts were. The process is almost, but not quite, circular—it is insular; that is, it results in insularity and a failure to establish the common ground that we regularly take to be a necessary condition of a genuine science.[7]

[7] *David Hume: Philosophical Historian*, David F. Norton and Richard M. Popkin, eds. (New York: Bobbs-Merrill, 1965), pp. xlviii-xlix.

There are other problems of a very practical sort, as Walter Kaufmann has pointed out, in claiming freedom from value biases. I will mention two. First, there is the fallacy of assuming that where "value-free" instruction exists, students will somehow learn on their own to apply the critical thinking they have been taught to use in academic subjects to social, political, and personal issues. Such a transfer cannot be assumed:

During the first third of this century the German universities could boast of a galaxy of distinguished scholars who applied the highest standards in their specialities and won a large number of Nobel Prizes. But their students did not learn to apply similar standards of rationality to moral and political questions, and Hitler was as popular with students and university-trained people as with less educated Germans.[8]

Second, a belief in any dichotomy between fact and value is misleading. The selection of subject matter, the interpretations and applications given it in the classroom—these and a score of other academic decisions are shot through with value judgments. To fail to acknowledge them and face this situation openly is to fool the dull students and make the bright ones cynical.

[8] Kaufmann, "Educational Development and Normative Philosophy," *Harvard Educational Review*, Summer, 1966, p. 262.

The Muscatine Report, presenting the findings of the Select Committee on Education, University of California, Berkeley, pointed out that this discrepancy between claim and action creates a credibility gap:

They [reform-minded students] find it hard to conceive that the purpose of the university can be to seek and preserve pure knowledge. They feel that impartiality cannot exist in the social sciences, or for that matter with any subject that deals with man and his culture. Instead of praising the impartiality of the teacher who does not relate his lesson to immediate problems, they accuse him of moral irresponsibility.[9]

Perceptive students see that the guise of objectivity is often used by faculty, and indeed by whole universities, not as a safeguard of truth but as a cover for inertia or vested interests. Professors and administrators sometimes assert that the university is not an instrument of direct social action at the very time that they show by contract research, course content, and a score of other developments that they are, in fact, state's men and that the university is engaged in action that directly serves the social status quo. By-products of the claim to certainty may be various forms of deception or a disposition to social detach-

[9] *Education at Berkeley: Report of the Select Committee on Education* (University of California, Berkeley, 1966), p. 34.

ment. The former can be the enemy of truth, the latter of honor. Both must go.

The mention of detachment brings us to a problem that causes trouble in one of our traditional divisions of learning, the humanities. It is the problem that the novelist John Barth has called the malady of *cosmopsis*—the paralysis of the undifferentiated cosmic view. In the natural sciences, learning is essentially sequential; there are certain prerequisites to later accomplishments, and an order of progression is important. Meanwhile, subject matter in the social and behavioral sciences is handled mainly in terms of linkages. This, that, and the other go together, with each discipline informing another and yet able to stand alone. It is in the humanities that learning is uniquely concentric.[10] Certain ideas, themes, and problems run through everything—types of human love, free will and determinism, theories of history, God, and man—and a person comes to them so often, from so many directions, encountering such an abundance of arguments for rival perspectives, that the result may be *cosmopsis*. It is the peril of knowing not too little but too much and, in "knowing" everything, having nothing that will serve to validate attitudes and deeds.

[10] I am endebted to Daniel Bell for this taxonomy. See Daniel Bell, *The Reforming of General Education* (New York: Columbia University Press, 1966), p. 141.

A philosophy of education appropriate for the next transformation of man, one that will serve as an alternative model, must be free of both the pretension to certainty that is sometimes found in the social sciences and the submission of too many in the humanities to extreme relativism. To live is to act, and we must have certitudes to provide bases for action. But because we are finite, these can be only provisional—there is no absolute certainty. To have certitudes gives us something on which to stand. To acknowledge their provisional nature keeps us humble and open to change.

An essential corollary of this alternate philosophy, when applied to education, is a commitment to the university as a center of independent thinking. A university at the mercy of societal forces, pushed and pulled by commercial and political interests, cannot achieve distinctive institutional character even provisionally.[11] Yet, at the same time, a university that uses autonomy as an excuse to draw away from the

---

[11] If anyone thinks that this freedom is assured in the present university, let him be informed by developments at the University of Hawaii. There President Thomas Hamilton notified, in 1967, an assistant professor of political science who was an outspoken opponent of the Vietnam war that he would not be retained on the faculty. And Hamilton's action was influenced, according to the *New York Times*, by the threat of the Waikiki Lions Club to march on the university unless this professor's contract was terminated. See *New York Times*, Sunday, June 11, 1967, p. 3.

world cannot have impact on it. Independence dare not mean isolation, because the next transformation of man will involve a world culture for the whole man. Yet, independence must mean free inquiry and independent thought if we are to effect a transformation.

Traditionally, church-related colleges and universities have been more disposed than have public institutions to strive for the "absolutes" or certitudes, the shared values, and the spirit of independence that can define and motivate a community of learning. But in earlier times church institutions erred on the side of rigidity, gaining spiritual security at the price of intelectual vigor. More recently, most such colleges and universities have gone over to the other extreme. Concerned for acceptability in the public domain, they now run the risk of substituting the empty mind for the closed one; in the area of educational philosophy they are, like many secular institutions, bland.

But to substitute vacuity for rigidity is no solution. We need other models, acknowledging, I suggest, the inevitability of value judgments and the provisional nature of all value judgments, the essentiality of institutional autonomy and yet the accountability of all institutions. These are emphases appropriate to our condition and our future. And, happily, there is evidence that a concern for these matters is spreading.

After a period in which theory was scorned and action emphasized, educators now are showing a new regard for theory. They see that action, energy, and effort are never ends in themselves but are always means unto something. Independently, certain current studies have found that of late campus leaders are giving institutional purposes a high priority; they now recognize them as crucial to the vitality, character, and distinctiveness of a campus.[12] The presence of definite objectives, in an atmosphere sufficiently open to provide opportunity for challenge to such objectives, make the best educational environment for student development.

Institutional objectives—understood as the "what" and "why" of a program, as opposed to instrumental strategies, the "how" and "when"—are not only basic to institutional character and a catalytic learning environment but are also indexes of institutional courage. To be different means risking action based on perspectives critical of the times. Thus, the measure of this form of distinctiveness, we may hypothesize, is the extent to which it breaks with established ways.

[12] Future of the Liberal Arts Colleges study, a project recently completed, directed by Morris Keeton, Academic Vice-President, Antioch College, Yellow Springs, Ohio. Institutional Distinctiveness and Student Development research project, in process at the Center for Research and Development in Higher Education, University of California, Berkeley.

There is also something to be said about the importance of distinctiveness for the achievement of educational reforms. It makes possible an appeal to a strong motive force now largely untapped—the motive of purpose. Under the terms of our present institutional model, with its emphasis on professionalism and guild standing, proposals for change must somehow be based on an appeal to faculty self-interest. But, of course, it is not really in the interest of the faculty, if there is only the one-model value system, to promote changes based on perspectives critical of established standards. Consequently, few radical innovations are being enacted. Those changes that are accepted are keyed more to efficiency than to idealism. Faculties are so conservative, in fact, that there is no better way to determine the extent to which a proposed change is radical than to test the extent of faculty opposition to it.

We may, however, again be at a turning point. The argument for faculty self-interest has reached its nadir. Enlightened self-interest has become in many cases raw selfishness. Faculty, living in and for themselves, find that they are easily bored and quickly jaded. No wonder. The educated life was never intended to bind a man in on himself. The self is too small a center for enduring satisfaction. Those maxims taught to students—know thyself, fulfill thyself, transcend thyself—also have relevance for faculty.

And faculty now may be ready to heed them. The appeal to purposes, to purposes that transcend the self, makes psychological and philosophical sense. Our challenge is to see that it makes sense for the world into which we are moving, for the whole man in a world culture.

CONFLICTS IN THE CURRICULUM

It is through the curriculum that institutional purposes are structured and transmitted to the learners. A curriculum is an instrumentality—not just of knowledge but of purposes. There are two problems that inhibit the effectiveness of our dominant curriculum model and keep it from being an instrumentality appropriate for the needs of students in the future. Consider first the problem caused by the fact that our present commitment to subject-matter specializations is in conflict with our commitment to educate the whole person. What we do, in effect, is to cut off the student's head from his body and have it dissected according to the specialties of various departments while the victim's body is allotted to student personnel services.[13]

[13] See Lloyd J. Averill, "Conscience and Competence: Christian Values in the Student Personnel Program," *Journal of Teacher Education*, (1963-1964), pp. 276-83.

No wonder there is so much confusion about what is meant when we talk of personalizing the educational experience. Faculty members usually mean that they want to make the disciplines relevant to the person. But students usually mean that they want to bring the total person to bear on the disciplines. There is a world of difference.

The second problem grows out of the first. Because role specialization militates against a holistic approach to the educational environment, we have a conflict caused by faculty emphasis on the intellectual liberation of the individual and his responsibility in the learning process, while student personnel services enforce parietal rules regulating the student's social and personal life. It is not surprising that those institutions emphasizing free inquiry and independent study are having trouble over social regulations. Students at such places recognize the incongruity of being given considerable freedom academically and being encouraged to believe that they have the maturity to handle any intellectual problem, while they remain bound by social regulations that are clearly a vote of "no confidence" in their ability to discipline themselves socially.

What could be done about these two problems?

Marshall McLuhan, a prophet of the electronic age, claims that our present subject-matter specializations are as antiquated as the trivium and quadrivium were at the time of the Renaissance.[14] Perhaps so. Certainly the academic "action" today is on the interface between the conventional disciplines, while the prospects for the future point to new learning configurations hardly recognizable by today's standards. Hence, curricula appropriate for the new man in the new age will need to be both more flexible and better integrated.

A start in that direction would be for us to cease the fratricidal war between general education and specialism. Specialization out of context produces only technique. General education without specificity is not relevant for life where it is lived. Either extreme assures the triumph of post-historic man. Instead of present practice, in which the curriculum builds on a general education that comes too early for mature understanding and emphasizes a specialism that comes too late to stir the student's emotions, we would do better to offer learning that features modes of conceptualization within disciplines and the fundamental issues in knowledge that underlie all disciplines. This would provide a cohesiveness across departments that is not present now, and encourage us to make the end of education a capacity for good judgment—the end, after all, to which all knowledge is the means. Thus the student's educa-

[14] McLuhan, *Understanding Media: The Extensions of Man* (New York: McGraw-Hill, 1965), p. 347.

tional experience would become more relevant and personal.

As for the problem of tensions created by intellectual freedom in the context of social restrictions, it can best be handled by reference to the third area where present practices are defective and in conflict with alternative modes that might better serve an education committed to the whole man in a world culture. I refer to the area of campus planning and facilities construction.

ENVIRONMENTAL ARCHITECTURE

Architecture both reflects and influences the values of any particular environment. It does so now on every campus. At most places, academic buildings are "zoned" according to the specifications of the various disciplines—the humanities complex, the social sciences buildings, and the various facilities for the natural sciences. This is true at the very time when the fortress of the disciplines, emphasizing fixed boundaries and an enclave mentality, has been shown to be inappropriate for the emphases of the nuclear-electronic age on multiple sensory mix, process, flexibility, and contingency. Most campus facilities are allies of dated thinking. They are a part of the impedimenta to change. We can excuse the planners of twenty-five to fifty years ago who zoned campuses in this way. They were conforming to ideas dictated by an expanding industrial society (although, even then, educational leaders of the stature of Alfred North Whitehead were warning of the dangers of rigid specialization[15]). But we can hardly show the same tolerance for campus planners now who continue the zoning style of construction despite the evidence that we are moving into a post-industrial epoch where space needs are going to be quite different from the past and where, in contrast, the ideas of the new environmental architecture have great contributions to make in setting up an educational milieu appropriate for the future.

Consider the consequences when architecture is kept in the service of archaism. Educational leaders acknowledge that the concept of *in loco parentis* is inappropriate for campus governance, in terms of the values modern youth bring to college and the educational purposes modern institutions of learning have for youth. But most residence halls, by their locations and interior arrangements, reflect the assumptions of that earlier and antiquated concept. Women are housed on one side of the campus and men on the other. Dormitories are constructed to facilitate control of student life rather than freedom and convenience. They illustrate how form follows function.

[15] Whitehead, *The Aims of Education and Other Essays* (New York: The Macmillan Company, 1959), p. 10.

But form also evokes function. Now, when the thinking for the future suggests the need for facilities that will be less like barracks and more like apartments, we ought to be on guard against building residence halls whose form evokes functions no longer relevant.

Another example of the effects of conventional specialistic zoning is the separation of social and residential buildings from those used for academic purposes. Almost every campus has residence halls, lounges, and the like "over there" and classrooms, labs, and other academic buildings "over here." Such conditions do not help students to integrate their emotional and intellectual development. There is need, I suggest, for alternative models that emphasize the total harmony of being and the unity of the total educational environment.

Reference to campus planning must include some comment on commercial athletics and automobiles. Mention is usually made of the space they take up and the aesthetic complications they create for the conscientious administrator. Or, although less often, we speak of the adverse effect commercialized sports and cars have on student study time and kindred academic priorities. But there is more to be said. Let me mention a situation that shows another way that commercialized athletics can influence the life of an institution.

A few years ago, at the University of the Pacific, 13 of the campus's 73 acres were taken up by a football stadium. In a city of under 100,000 population, with a university of less than 3,000 students, the stadium seated over 30,000. No doubt when the stadium was built there seemed to be plenty of space for such a pleasurable extravagance. But before long the city of Stockton moved in close around the campus, the university itself expanded, and the resultant space pressure influenced the university's decision to crowd the buildings for three cluster colleges and their 750 residential students into another 13-acre site. Academic programs operating all the regular school year were assigned space about equivalent to that of a stadium used only a fraction of the year. Alas, how the sins of the fathers extend to the second and third generation.

As for the automobile problem, the best comprehensive attempt I know of, both to limit the number of cars on campus and to bring cars, roads, and parking lots to terms with the natural setting, is at the University of California, Santa Cruz. The isolated location of that campus creates special problems in this connection for the chancellor and his staff but, to date, what they are doing is a harbinger of hope.

While there are some bright features in the architecture at Santa Cruz and a few other places, most of the new campuses being developed across the country are a cause for gloom. Given the opportunities of our day, we ought to develop learning environments based more on dissimilarity than similarity with the existing model, but most of what we see is familiar, safe, and repetitive. We may take encouragement from a few exciting architectural probes, such as the Robert Hutchins Goddard Library, Clark University, but the rest seldom qualify as even new means to traditional ends. There are too few fresh ideas, and those we have are not being exploited.

One of the best, an idea that holds potential for the testing of alternative models within established universities and one about which I shall have more to say later, is the cluster college concept. Unfortunately, to date, cluster colleges are developing along disciplinary lines, or as attempts to recapture an old liberal arts college ethos. And facilities being constructed for them reflect these commitments. But the concept could be turned to alternate and perhaps better ends. For example, there is a growing realization among educators that the modern university has not effectively accepted the challenges of the urban setting in which it is often located and to which it must relate. Separatist and elitist notions still dominate the style and focus of campus life, even in urban schools. Concerning these matters, John W. Gardner has written:

The city is the heart and brain of an industrial society. But our cities today are plagued with every conceivable ill: apathy, crime, poverty, racial conflict, slum housing, air and water pollution, inadequate schools and hospitals, and a breakdown in transportation. Coping with those problems is going to be very near the top of the national agenda for the next decade. There are no institutions better equipped to serve as a base for that struggle than the colleges and universities, but they have played a negligible role thus far. The strategic role played by the land-grant universities in developing American agriculture and the rural areas has no parallel in the cities.[16]

The University of Illinois, Congress Circle, Chicago, is an expression of the interest in having a state university located at the epicenter of modern life, the city. But it is not enough to locate students on a large, self-contained campus, even though that location brings them into proximity with social and political realities. Such a campus can still be a cocoon. Something more is needed to educate students for good "city-zenship."

The cluster college idea, turned not toward the establishment of old-fashioned programs in new facilities at cloistered locations but toward programs focused on urban problems and set in strategically located city buildings—perhaps commercial sites—

---

[16] Gardner, *Agenda for the Colleges and Universities* (New York: Academy for Educational Development), Paper No. 1, p. 7.

might be a way to transform the way we think about "town-gown relationships" and at the same time open up new educational options for new times. The intent would not be to bring such colleges to terms with urban realities—that suggests accommodation with existing conditions—but to bring them to face forms of reality that could motivate them to work to achieve something better for urban society.

Additional evidence that we are boxed in by single-model thinking is seen in the priorities usually set for the physical development of our campuses. Lacking new visions, we work at building what has been done before, our contribution being to build it bigger and better. Since, for example, prestige in the past has been associated with libraries and labs, we continue the tradition. So, at Notre Dame, Cal Tech, Hofstra, and other schools, there are newly completed, multi-storied libraries costing millions of dollars. They are better than the past at its best, but their form and spirit help to solidify commitments that belong to the past—to linear learning, to centralization, to exactitude more than flexibility. Such edifices, in the emerging electronic age, may turn out to be monuments to antiquity, high-rise hitching posts in a world that has moved on.

While research libraries and manuscript repositories will, of course, be necessary for the emerging culture, books of this sort could be housed in existing facilities on most campuses if general library expansion were met in new ways. The needs of the majority of undergraduate students could be satisfied by paperback libraries distributed around a campus, operating without much concern for the problems of replacement and duplication. Half the price of one of our monolithic library buildings would buy functional space and thousands of books for a long time. Some variation of this scheme might serve us now, at least until we learn more about what the electronic media mean for this aspect of university life.

Or, as another option, some of the money designated for a big library might be joined with the money slated for the construction of a conventional dormitory to build instead a study-residence complex, featuring living room–bedroom–bath suites for students and with study lounges and libraries scattered throughout. Thus, we would avoid construction of a dormitory that we know is already obsolete and a library that may become obsolete, in favor of a building that integrates and personalizes a student's activities—plus, not incidentally, providing an answer to the parietal rules problem since, presumably, students would have keys to their suites and could entertain guests in their living rooms. In this plan, insights of environmental architecture would also be applied, insights suggested by the architectural designer John M. Johansen: "As buildings become looser assemblages, less finite and static, they will become volatile, will reach out and fuse with adjoining buildings and lose their identity in a continual froth of space-form." [17]

It could be the same with laboratories and classroom buildings. Flexibility is now more important than exactitude. Mausoleums like the life sciences building at Berkeley must not be duplicated. That building sits so heavily on its site that it will always be for me a symbol of man's desire for permanence gone dogmatic.

There are other urgencies about our situation now that support the case for an intensification of the search for alternative models—philosophical, curricular, architectural. One is that unparalleled physical expansion seems inevitable. So many students will be in college by 1975, economist Peter F. Drucker has calculated, that housing them will require erecting facilities equal to twice all the campus buildings constructed in the three hundred years since Harvard was founded.[18] We are going to build. But must we build as we have built?

Dissatisfaction with current educational arrangements has grown until it just about parallels, in scope

[17] Johansen, "An Architecture for the Electronic Age," *The American Scholar*, Summer, 1960, p. 469.
[18] Drucker, *Bricks and Mortarboards* (New York: Educational Facilities Laboratories, 1964), p. 7.

and intensity, the need for future expansion. The voices of dissent—minority voices to be sure, but the future is always shaped by minorities—make us wonder about the adequacy of what has been done. In the last two decades we have hired good administrators and architects, and paid huge sums of money for campus facilities, programs and development, faculty salaries, and student services. Furthermore, we have tried to adhere to the values of our prevailing model and in most cases have achieved good success by its standards. Yet there exists a deep anxiety about the meaning of it all.

The educated are physically comfortable but not very happy; healthy in body but less so in mind, and still less in spirit; active, efficient, articulate, but not especially purposeful. There is clearly the need to think again about what men ought to live for, about our assumptions, values, and objectives, in order better to decide what sort of places we want to live in and within what arrangements we want to work.

Lewis Mumford's challenge is for us to be content with nothing less than a revolutionized culture, one nourished "not only by a new vision of the whole, but a new vision of a self capable of understanding and cooperating with the whole." [19] To take up that challenge would be a way, as education becomes the

[19] Mumford, *The Transformations of Man*, p. 134.

principal business of life, for the principle business of those in education to become the development of a total educational environment which would bring to human activities the quality of significance. It would mean radical reforms, to be sure, but it would also give us the sense of purpose needed to direct coming changes toward the goal of unified man.

II

RESOURCES FOR
COMPREHENSIVE INNOVATION

The creation of viable alternative models for higher education, I have hypothesized, would open the way for the reforms necessary to make colleges and universities centers of leadership in the next historic transformation of man. Reforms of a substantial sort are called for, not so much because the past was bad, but because the future is going to be markedly different. Therefore, among the divergent options to be set up, there ought to be examples of comprehensive innovation or holistic experimentation, models of new means to new ends. Establishing these would be unquestionably difficult, given the dominance of that one model, the "versity," in which there is a disinclination to accept new means even to traditional ends. Nevertheless, changes external to education now compel us to explore possibilities for radical changes within education no matter how formidable the odds against them.

I am prepared to contend that certain developments in our colleges and universities are, in fact, resources for innovation; and rather than playing the game of referral-deferral—in which administrators, faculty, and trustees each contend that their interest group is friendly to change but is blocked by the opposition of one or more of the other groups—we should take up these resources and proceed to utilize them in achieving examples of comprehensive reformation. But what is going on that might be turned to our advantage?

The most significant development in higher education over the last twenty years is not the introduction of computer-assisted instruction, nor the expansion of federal funding and federal influence, nor the rise of institutional consortia, nor growth in numbers, facilities, and other things of this sort. The development of greatest consequence has been in the realm of the mind and the spirit and has to do with ideas and personalities; it is the emerging essentialist-existentialist confrontation. What we decide about this matter, which involves our basic assumptions and purposes, will determine what we do with all other developments; and furthermore, within it are the dynamics for comprehensive innovation.

Because this essentialist-existentialist confrontation

in education is being duplicated in many realms of contemporary life, a field of endeavor reaching from academe to industry will be used to illustrate the issue that we face. The structure housing Yale's School of Art and Architecture is the work of Paul Rudolph, an architect who has of late been challenging the *status quo* in his field. Opponents say that his building, an example of environmental architecture, doesn't work—rooms are too large or too small, not functional, and have an excess of gadgets, crannies, levels, and other eccentric surprises. Adhering to the values of an industrial age, they judge the building in terms of efficiency—"rentable footage per dollar invested" is the commercial expression of the point.

Advocates of Rudolph's work say that straightarrow functionalism ignores the fact that art should stimulate the emotions as well as the mind. What a building does to a personality is more important than the way the building implements a person's work. Thus, "Rudolph's involvement with technological function is always a secondary matter. His intuitive approach is based on ability to stir senses with his now-infinite and now-confining spaces." [1] Unpredictability, angularity, an emphasis on texture, color, and drama, even playfulness—these are the characteristics

[1] David Jacobs, "The Rudolph Style: Unpredictable," *New York Times Magazine*, March 26, 1967, p. 57.

of a style that this architect has termed "the new freedom." [2]

The formal versus the vital—that is the issue at the heart of the essentialist-existentialist confrontation, whether the field of encounter be architecture or education. And this is the issue that we must understand.

Essentialists in education are formalists who reach back over time to the ancient Greeks—from Wittgenstein and Russell, Dewey and James, Hegel and Kant, Mill and Bentham, back through Locke, Descartes, Calvin, Aquinas, Augustine, to Aristotle and Plato—and behind them to "timeless" essences. Whether idealists, emphasizing ideas and forces that transcend the particulars of human existence, or realists, concentrating on men and affairs in and of this world, essentialists are concerned for that which goes beyond time and place—for that which is permanent, uniform, rational, sure. For some, the standard by which all else is judged is God; for others, nature or humanity; but never is it that solitary being—man.

The existentialists, on the other hand, center their attention on man as man. Buber, Heidegger, Sartre, and Camus all see philosophy and education as efforts to give rational form to a vision that must be, finally, intensely personal. Only so can it be vital. And behind them, for they too have honorable ante-

[2] *Ibid.*

cedents, are Kierkegaard, Pascal, Rousseau, Montaigne, Augustine (it is possible to have a foot in each camp), Tertullian, Socrates, and Job.

When Socrates acted as an intellectual gadfly to his fellow Athenians, asking questions that challenged assumptions, bidding citizens to determine individually what they believed, emphasizing the process of investigation more than the acquisition of knowledge, he was a forerunner of existentialism.

When Augustine spoke through the *City of God*, he showed himself to be a Neoplatonist bent on reconciling the world of men with that of God. But when he revealed himself in the *Confessions*, personally, spiritually, he was then a man confronted by God, a human being who could tremble as well as testify.

Pascal looked at man during the ascendancy of seventeenth-century rationalism, yet he saw only a confused and confusing creature; he looked to the heavens at a time of confidence in natural law and saw contradiction and ambiguity. That man existed in time, space, and history was certain, but what sort of being man was to become could be for Pascal only a matter of faith.

The irrational in man, and yet man's primacy over all rational systems; the threat of every system to each fumbling, erratic, imperfect man—these were Kierkegaard's themes, just as they are existentialist concerns and existential problems yet. Today the system's essential component is technique—defined as "any complex of standardized means for attaining a predetermined result."[3] Technique unerringly achieving programmed results means, in education, that it is not the person in and for himself who is being educated, but a person trained in and for the system. Thus means become ends, and processes become absolutized. To absolutize an instrumentality is indeed the end, for it compels one to live on an endless treadmill.

The quest for meanings is crucial for existentialists. Some say that man creates all meanings. Sartre: ". . . every man, without any support or help whatever, is condemned at every instant to invent man."[4] Viktor Frankl represents another perspective in saying that existence is not invented by man, but rather detected.[5] Either way, not media but meanings make the message.

It did not take Marshal McLuhan to discover that media shape the messages they bring, and in fact contribute thereto. Others made these points much earlier. McLuhan's unique "contribution" is in as-

[3] Robert K. Merton, Introduction to Jacques Ellul's *The Technological Society* (New York: Alfred A. Knopf, 1965), p. vi.

[4] Jean-Paul Sartre, *Existentialism and Humanism* (London: Methuen, 1948), p. 34.

[5] Frankl, *Man's Search for Meaning* (New York: Washington Square Press, 1963), p. 154.

signing certain characteristics that are now evident in the young—their interest in participation by aural, tactile, and kinetic experiences; their attraction to color, texture, and new experiential configurations that unite the full human sensorium—to the impact of the electronic media. This is the message he attributes to television and other mechanisms of the new electronic age. McLuhan is right, of course, about the radical changes in the tastes and values of the young. He is wrong, however, in thinking that these changes are due to particular media. McLuhan has spotted the effect but missed the cause. The "turned on" generation has been flipped, not by an electric switch but by a panexistential ethos that challenges youth to look within themselves, to feel things deeply, and to insist on meanings in life that are personal and vital.

Existentialism on campus is most evident among the young; yet, beware of identifying the sides in the present struggle on the basis of superficial markings. This confrontation is not between gray flannel suits and beards, nor between people this side or that side of age thirty. You cannot bag people like groceries. There are, however, certain emphases that go far deeper than any surface differences, values that differentiate the combatants, and these can be listed.

Essentialists in education contend that there is a specific body of knowledge to be taught and learned, that human nature is the same in every epoch, that tradition and ceremony, history and experience, are worthy teachers. So subject matter and standards, prerequisites and sequences, are essentialists' concerns, as are the disciplines and the departmental style of life.

Educational change, for most essentialists, is possible so long as continuity is not sacrificed to immediacy, so long as anomalies are not used to justify anarchy. They are not persuaded, however, that the present clamor for change bespeaks a bona fide crisis in education. They say with the English: "When it is not necessary to change, it is necessary not to change."

An essentialist extreme is illustrated by the annual deluge of books by academics that are, in the familiar word, "competent." Critical reviews begin, "This is a competent book," and end, "One wonders why he took the trouble to write it." Such works are faithfully accurate, well organized, in the proper style, and quite harmless—save for the cost to the writer and reader in energy, curiosity, zest, concern, and whatever else they brought to that literary encounter and lost there.

Essentialists are also likely to be conspicuous in making academic freedom a matter of conceptual entities—definitions, mechanisms for implementation, and penalties for violations. Existentialists, on the other hand, are more likely to see academic freedom as a relational condition obtaining among persons. But their lack of emphasis on form, in this connection or others, doesn't mean that freedom is any less important to them. Indeed, the existentialist's rallying cry is the "new freedom."

From the time of the sixteenth century, as William Barrett, Ernest Becker, and other writers are emphasizing, Western man has been moving out of the medieval matrix—that complex of church-state arrangements by which all of man's life was dignified and controlled—into a position of increasing autonomy. Now, stripped of his traditional consolations, man stands naked and alone, thrilled by his freedom, but terrified too. Absolute certainties are gone; only provisional certitudes remain. But these are enough, existentialists argue, if man can develop a tolerance for ambiguity. Indeed, it may be in this area that his strengths should be developed. The only advantage the human mind has over the computer is its ability to work with vague, ambiguous, even contradictory problems. In past centuries, to maintain human supremacy over the environment, man utilized his brain to unscramble complex issues. In the future, supremacy may depend on his ability to scramble things up again—making work for man that the computers cannot handle.

More seriously, existentialists are less concerned

about continuity with the past than about present and personal relevance. For them, as with Augustine, there is only a present of things past, a present of things present, and a present of things to come. And this continuum is judged by the free man of flesh and blood, creature of mind and spirit, the one with the unique capacity for self-awareness and sensitivity.

André Gide has claimed that the chief attraction of Montaigne is his willingness to examine himself and reveal himself openly. "In every historical period," Gide wrote,

an attempt is made to cover over this real self with a conventional figure of humanity. Montaigne pushes aside this mask in order to get at what is essential; if he succeeds it is thanks to assiduous efforts and singular perspicacity; it is by opposing convention, established beliefs, conformism, with a spirit of criticism that is constantly on the alert, easy and at the same time tense, playful, amused at everything, smiling, indulgent yet uncompromising, for its object is to know and not to moralize.[6]

The new existentialism, panexistentialism, breaks with the dark, dank mood of Kierkegaard, Heidegger, and other somber representatives of the philosophy. The emphasis now is on the Montaigne manner and on the full range of human experiences from which

[6] Gide, *Montaigne* (New York: McGraw-Hill, 1964), p. 3.

meanings are derived—disorder and order, mystery and certitudes, frailty and aspiration, grief and joy. There is an interest, for example, in historical perspective but not in historicism. Existentialists agree with Gibbon that the study of the classics may have retarded rather than hastened the intellectual development of the West. Men used the past as a fixed model rather than a stimulus to model building. "The authority of the ancients, and of Aristotle in particular, drove culture into a rut and during the sixteenth century the University of Paris turned out almost nothing but bookworms and pedants." [7]

It is to avoid such a fate, without ignoring history, that existentialists emphasize that instruction and involvement are both facets of the learning process. Essentialist pedagogy has stressed the accumulative side; now existentialists stress the affective. It is a matter of offering, on the one hand, something to be learned, while on the other it is an interest in how the learner takes the learning. So, to existentialists, what is said in class by the professor becomes less important than what is heard by the student. The number of lectures given, the amount of material covered, and the procedures and arrangements employed are significant only to the extent that they help students find self-identity and develop good judgment. The

[7] *Ibid.*, p. 7.

methodology of existentialists is provisional but operational. Their style is often improvisational. But what they lose in efficiency, they hope to make up in vitality.

THE ESSENTIALIST-EXISTENTIALIST CONFRONTATION AND THE INNOVATIVE PROCESS

Because the essentialist-existentialist confrontation is the dominant feature in the present educational environment, it is certain that proposals for changes are being affected by it. Innovations are almost never decided on their merits.[8] They are initiated, sustained, and finally terminated by considerations external to the proposals themselves. This is why it is so important to view the process of innovation in the context of the prevailing situation. Only so can we determine what is possible.

The climate of learning in the House of Intellect today is influenced mainly by the essentialists. They set the thermostat, but their efforts at climate control are being increasingly disrupted by existentialists who keep opening windows to let in fresh air. Teaching assistants and some assistant professors, those

[8] *Innovation in Education*, Matthew Miles, ed. (New York: Bureau of Publications, Teachers College, 1964), p. 635.

whose memories of stifling classrooms are most vivid, are especially active among these fresh air fiends. So are people in some areas of the humanities. Yet even there, and certainly in the other divisions of learning, the essentialists, although harassed, are still the masters of the house—albeit increasingly grumpy hosts.

Now, in these times of disquietude and testing, brought about largely by radical changes external to education—particularly the shift into a post-industrial, nuclear-electronic epoch—it is not surprising that there is a broad-based interest in innovation. However, since the essentialists are in control, we may predict that the following types of change have the best prospect for success. First, there are those changes that show good innovation-system congruence—defined as how well the innovation fits in with existing institutional practices. An illustration is the establishment of Justin Morrill College at Michigan State University. This liberal arts program, set up under administrative impetus to begin operation in 1965, is commissioned to be innovative to the extent of bringing students and faculty into closer and more active working relationships and providing greater flexibility in the ways university requirements can be met—all to the end of making the students' learning experience more personal and relevant. However, the calendar, costs, admissions criteria, course distribution requirements, faculty appointments, and salaries have been made to conform to general university standards. Complementarity, not confrontation, is the rule. To be different without being special is the goal. At Justin Morrill there is good innovation-system congruence. This is the kind of change essentialists can support.

A second kind of change and one likely to succeed, given the control of essentialists, is the soft-shoe innovation. Not all the essentials for essentialists have to do with underlying values or organizational overlay. An innovator may succeed as much by good manners as by brilliant ideas—if he is a "good fellow" with a courteous, patient, generous, predictable personality; or has "good credentials," a Ph.D. bestowed by one of a coterie of elect schools, and not just publications nor even professional writings, but research publications featuring "hard" data. Moreover, if he has "an appreciation for the realities," that is, a tolerance for the static; and agrees to "live within prescribed means"—abide by the pinched vision of an atrophied brain-trust—even though, as McGeorge Bundy said, excessive caution may be bad management; and if, in sum, our innovator is a "team man," a committee type who blends into the woodwork or wallpaper—either straight grain or flower pattern, depending on the setting—then we may free him to experiment. And we need not fear the results.

Structural congruence in innovations and personal

compatability for innovators are requirements essentialists impose on change to assure that tradition will control experimentation. They want this, not because they are weak or habit-bound, but because their values dictate such control. Values determine standards, and by such standards all changes are judged. Therefore, the innovative process today is characterized by changes reached by consensus and implemented with a minimum of tension and risk, changes that sustain the status quo by conforming to prevailing values.

Where will members of the "loyal opposition," the existentialists, apply their power? What sort of innovations will they support? Existentialists, given their values, may be expected to favor curriculum variations that show promise of freeing the individual from the dominance of the institution—independent study, the use of nonintellective variables in the selection of students and the evaluation of their work, and the community concept of academic governance. They are likely to favor proposals that break open the conventional packaging of knowledge. The times, they think, call for new learning contexts. The students stand to benefit by an alternate problem-theme approach, and the faculties need the stimuli of new assignments.

Professors in increasing numbers are bored. They teach in a perfunctory fashion, not because they don't know any better but because they aren't motivated enough to do better. Their boredom is the expression of the human psyche's compensation for the fatigue that comes to those who are caught between competing loyalties. Faculty commissioned to teach have also been conditioned to seek satisfaction through tighter and tighter specialization. Such specialized subject matter can be taught to an undergraduate, but at the sacrifice of comprehension by the student if the job is done at a level of sophistication sufficient to sustain the professor's interest. The options for faculty are, too often, exclusive association with like-minded specialists or boredom with the unmindful students. Existentialists press for problem-theme, transdisciplinary courses or, at least, for cross discipli-nary courses. Such programs are seen as more flexible for students and as valuable in bringing faculty out to the borders of their disciplines where boredom gives way before the challenges of a new relationship. Existentialists are, in addition, responsive to those ideas that propel the free individual into social and political situations where man is pitted against the machine or the Establishment.

Proposals for change from existentialists are likely to be more radical in content and less predictable in style than those of the essentialists. Not only is their vitality hard to encapsulate, even as individuality is difficult to routinize, but existentialists often allow their antipathy toward organizations to encourage ignorance thereof. They may not know enough about institutional grids to realize how change might properly be effected. And to their ignorance they couple impatience—a most dangerous union, one likely to produce a bastard who becomes hysterical because he thinks that he has no legitimate connection with the past, or a messianic who thinks that the salvation of the world rests with him alone.

This, then, is our situation: Pressures for changes in education which have been building up from sources external to the campus, particularly those associated with the nuclear-electronic revolution, have now been joined and strengthened by the support of certain elements within the educational system —by some faculty and students and even a handful of administrators who see the contradictions inherent in the dominant model. This development has led to widespread curiosity about innovation and, in some places, to an essentialist-existentialist confrontation on the nature and extent of change.

Since the need, I contend, is for the establishment of alternative models, and especially for some that promise comprehensive innovation, the future is challenging for administrators and faculty who can view this situation with penetration and scope, for those who can think inclusively about the prospects for inclusive innovation.

To think inclusively means, first, to be aware that the present climate of learning is influenced by the essentialist-existentialist confrontation, to appraise the strengths and weaknesses of both sides, and to enlist the skills of both in attaining desired goals.

Second, to think inclusively is to see things from the other person's side without forgetting one's own perspective. To those who say that there is no reason to change, that there is nothing new under the sun, that human nature is the same forever, and that the old ways are the best ways, the inclusive innovator points out the need for other models by emphasizing the radical nature of the world into which we are moving. It is a world antithetical to the atomization the old technology produced, in which education was patterned after the industrial production line: a school was a "plant"; students, "products"; and learning, "training." The youth in this changing society are a new breed of cat in a different jungle, and there is some trailblazing to be done.

Then there are people who claim that change is impossible. Many in the radical left feel a sense of futility now. The Establishment is, they say, corrupt but resilient; it has devised ways to envelop criticism, absorb its impact without being affected, and go on as before.

Many educators share this pessimism toward the prospects for change, especially for educational institutions. The inclusive innovator, however, while aware of the problems, is not willing to concede that bureaucratic forms always block innovation or that hoary tradition frustrates all change. Changes do occur. In A.D. 1215, the papal legate in Paris forbade teachers to lecture on Aristotle's works; in 1231, Pope Gregory IX appointed a commission to expurgate him; by 1260, Aristotle had become *de rigueur* in every European university, and ecclesiastical councils penalized deviations from his views. This about-face for the church, that most conservative institution, occurred in just fifty years. Speaking of that length of time, the domination of graduate programs and subject matter specializations in our colleges and universities—perhaps the only institutions whose conservatism rivals that of the church—dates back only to 1876 and the founding of Johns Hopkins. From that beginning followed profound changes for all of education. But it doesn't always take fifty years. The nation's spasm over Sputnik in 1957 produced innovations in mathematics, science, and language instruction. The multiversities have come into prominence within the last decade, as have faculties. They enjoy salaries and benefits that put them among the social elite, while residual power in the nation-state shifts over to them as they provide technological expertise. Or, if education is impervious to change, what about the convulsion that Berkeley has undergone since 1964? In three years reform leaders there achieved changes—as, in a few months, did a new governor. Contrary to the popular notion, colleges and universities, like other institutions, are vulnerable to pressure, responsive to leadership, and in the process of important changes.

The third component of inclusive thinking is an appreciation for the dynamics of change in complex organizations. As theorists on social change have shown, successful innovations usually depend on the following factors: an ideology that motivates and unifies; a viable social matrix, showing certain features complementary with the innovation and others that challenge through contrast; strong leadership, the change agent; effective carrying mechanisms by which the proposed change is advanced; and finally a provision for self-renewal and critical analysis—self-renewal because innovators get discouraged (the flesh is willing but the spirit weakens) and critical analysis because all efforts at change are subject to attrition or compromise over time and therefore must be constantly reaffirmed or updated.

While philosophical scope, perspective on options, and an appreciation for the way change can be structured in complex organizations are all necessary parts of thinking inclusively, there is another side to the work of the innovator we need today. He not only thinks inclusively, he also forms inclusive innovations.

If one axiom on innovations is that they are initiated from the outside, a second is that they are most often too little and too late. The usual procedure is to make a gesture and a bow suffice for a movement toward reform. We profess to be attracted to independent study, for example, and so we arrange for perhaps one fourth of the student's schedule to be set up accordingly. Yet we keep up the regular schedule and its pressure in the rest of the student's program—and then regret that he doesn't do better with independent study. How many faculty members with one fourth of their term work load free for research, and three fourths tightly scheduled, get much writing done?

Partial, piecemeal innovation is, I suppose, better than none. It may open up a vision of possibilities. But it is quite evident that there is a paucity of radical change in higher education at a time when the conviction grows that radical change is called for. That is why inclusive innovation is the kind that really matters now, and why we must find innovators with the courage and audacity to try it. Architect Paul Rudolph is planning a complete community, Stafford, a Washington, D. C., satellite town. We need more educators thinking as comprehensively.

Immanuel Kant once denounced the inadequacies

of the science of the nineteenth century in the following way:

> I do not wish to hide the fact that I can only look with repugnance . . . upon the puffed-up pretentiousness of those volumes filled with wisdom, such as are fashionable nowadays. For I am fully satisfied that . . . the accepted methods must endlessly increase these follies and blunders, and that even the complete annihilation of all these fanciful achievements could not possibly be as harmful as this fictitious science with its accursed fertility.[9]

In the realm of education, Kant's words could be spoken by most of those of us committed to innovation and experimentation in American colleges and universities. We do not hide our repugnance for the pretentiousness of conventional educational arrangements, nor do we hesitate to point out the needless increase in follies and blunders that emanate from them as the fruit of their accursed fertility.

However, we also should take from Kant's actions a warning for our own. From our vantage point a hundred years beyond Kant, we see that this great philosopher, who proposed to correct the failures of the past and secure philosophy's future, in fact proceeded not only to sit upon the dung heap of those

[9] Immanuel Kant, quoted in Karl Popper, *The Open Society and Its Enemies*, Vol. I: *The Spell of Plato* (New York: Harper Torchbooks, 1962), p. 1.

philosophies for which he professed to feel repugnance but, alas, by his own efforts contributed mightily to its bulk.

Let us hope that we can learn something from history, and show magnanimity toward others and modesty about our own efforts as we try to advance the innovative process in the present climate of learning. But if we are destined to repeat history, we would do better to emulate the boldness of Job and, sitting upon our dunghill, steadfastly proclaim before God and man that the developing confrontation between essentialists and existentialists is itself a catalyst for change and that out of it may come innovators who think inclusively and press always toward comprehensive innovation.

III

CLUSTER COLLEGES
AS ALTERNATIVE MODELS

No problem exercises educational leaders more these days than the problem of size—large size. The public confidence in education and the contribution which education has made to the public have produced a growth pattern that now threatens to expand the modern university into an institutional Gargantua, albeit one devoid of the humanistic ideas of Rabelais' hero. Educators who believe that impersonality is a corollary of size say that if this problem is to be solved, we must devise new organizational arrangements which retain the benefits of large, diversified universities and at the same time revive those humanistic values traditionally associated with small liberal arts colleges.

The most promising solution yet advanced calls for the establishment of small colleges within the general framework of a large university. The advantages of the complex university may thus be coupled with the advantages of the unitary college: specialization and research can be fostered while undergraduates receive integrative, perhaps cross-disciplinary, learning experiences in a setting that renders education personal. This scheme is a harbinger of hope—for these and additional reasons.

Cluster colleges offer a way to change and improve institutions of learning by giving a new twist to the ancient maxim "divide and conquer." They may be expected to divide the masses of students into groups small enough to encourage identity and participation, thereby creating, as an additional benefit, a way for the absolute size of the university to increase while the working units remain small. And more, they should help to conquer that student apathy and hostility which grow out of a sense of powerlessness, by encouraging student involvement with the faculty in testing innovations, thus creating in the university a mechanism for institutional change without sacrificing tradition and order.

But more important than any of these reasons for the establishment of cluster colleges is the potential the concept has for the development and testing of holistic alternative models that may prove appropriate for the future of higher education. At a time when a few prestigious universities set the academic style for all the rest, the cluster college idea encourages the hope that these vanguard institutions might spin off colleges commissioned to innovate radically. Such colleges would have sufficient autonomy to dare to be different, precisely because participants therein would know that their security was assured by the fact they were operating under the umbrella of respectability provided by the sponsoring university. Change would have a chance as the principle of growth through diversity is applied in the centers of academic power.

Changes in the radical-model colleges could well follow two tracks—organizational or structural variations and diversity in value orientation. Universities could in these ways test alternatives to the present organizational bureaucracy and value conformity.

Admittedly, cluster colleges presently operating are not going as far as is here proposed. They show some interest in achieving organizational distinctiveness but little interest in distinctiveness at the level of values. It is a difference familiar to contemporary organization theory, the difference between changing "the processes *within* the system and the processes of change *of* the system."[1] Three characteristics now typify cluster college programs and they are all con-

[1] Talcott Parsons, "The Problems of the Theory of Change," in *The Planning of Change*, Bennis, Berne, and Chin, eds. (New York: Holt, Rinehart & Winston, 1961), p. 215.

cerned with changes in the processes within systems.

Existent cluster colleges, first, have initiated academic innovations which encourage independent study, student-formed seminars, tutorials, modified community government, closer student-faculty working relations, and academic calendar variations. Curriculum revisions such as problem-theme courses, the "three-tier" plan of study, and other action-oriented changes of the conventional ordering of both general education and specialization are also in evidence.

A second characteristic shared by cluster colleges, again with variations, is a residential arrangement in which facilities and programs combine to keep the student in the climate of learning. Faculty studies, seminar rooms and classrooms, even faculty apartments are often in or near dorms, Oxford and Cambridge style, with the intent to encourage vital academic relationships and aid in the achievement of the spirit of community. The planners believe, with Aristotle, that the happiness of man is best achieved in the life of a community. So, all-college activities such as "High Table" dinners or "College Night" are held, not only to enhance the academic and aesthetic contacts but also to encourage community by bringing college personnel together in a shared enterprise.

Another feature of cluster college development is the concern for some measure of autonomy within the sponsoring university. Actual administrative arrangements vary greatly among institutions, yet wherever these colleges exist there is tension between the necessity for loyalty to the parent institution and the need for freedom to innovate. Such tension is inevitable. Innovations are, after all, explicit or implied criticisms of the status quo. Many of the themes emphasized in cluster colleges—identity, relevance, involvement—are those of the systems shakers. The more radical the program, the more the college becomes an attempt to institutionalize anti-institutionalism. And the hazards are as great as the tensions are inevitable. Norman Birnbaum said, "Hell hath no fury like a vested interest scorned." A maxim for innovators as they strive to establish a working relationship with the personnel of the general university might be: Relate to establish confidence, in confidence establish autonomy.

It may be because this issue of autonomy and accountability is so explosive and complex that there is such a dearth of radical thinking in present cluster college planning. Many proposals are hardly more than house plans, ways of handling masses of students so as to minimize impersonality—elaborate recipes most noteworthy for cutting the pie bite-size. Even where more substantial innovations are introduced, the changes are often nostalgic attempts to recapture a lost small-college ethos and an old liberal

73

arts curriculum. It is almost as though the promoters adopted these themes for no better reason than that these were the sorts of changes faculty might be expected to permit in an ancillary program, as a way of assuaging their guilt for having long since abandoned such emphases in their own departments. Of course there are other and better reasons for the curricula of these small colleges, but there is no denying that political realities compromise the extent of change.

The universities sponsoring cluster colleges are accustomed to growth but are not necessarily friendly to innovation. Established institutions with proud traditions, they know that change is not synonymous with gain, and they are not prepared to repudiate the past in the name of novelty. If there is to be change, the tendency of the university is to structure it so that tradition controls innovation.

To illustrate: the criteria for the hiring and rank-promotion of faculties for the cluster colleges already in operation are, almost without exception, those used in the older colleges and schools of the "innovating" university. This is the way, we are told, to assure that the participants in the new college will not be regarded as second-rate, and that their work will be first-rate. But the criteria for placement and advancement are publications, contract research, professional mobility, guild standing, and other emphases that helped to create the problems that have, in turn, produced the rising disaffection with our schools. A legitimate interest in standards has prompted the imposition of the criteria, but these criteria work against the changes needed to satisfy the concerns that initially precipitated the idea for cluster colleges.

It is proper for a university to insist that all parts of the institution maintain high standards of scholarship, but it is institutional solipsism to conclude that such standards can be maintained only by conformity to arrangements operating in the older units. If the creation of small colleges in large universities is to be more than an opportunity for architectural audacity or schemes for the duplication of administrators and the expansion of budgets; if the new colleges are to be innovative at the point of basic university reforms; it is evident that more radical planning is needed. The search for distinctiveness is an invitation to new directions.

The point at which to begin, in order to make the cluster concept into a mechanism for the exploration of alternative models, is with the assertion that the weight of inertia in the university being what it is and the need for change being urgent, the establishment of cluster colleges shall be permitted only if the planners can show that the program and style of the college will be not just innovative, concerned with achieving established goals by new means, but un-apologetically experimental, in search of new goals by new means for new times. Innovation should be possible in conventional programs. Experimentation is the challenge for cluster colleges.

The history of higher education shows that new innovative colleges are seldom more experimental than in the first period of idealism and energy, after which changes tend back toward tradition. This is another reason for cluster colleges to reach for an identity based more on dissimilarities than on duplication. The parent institutions must give them sufficient autonomy to achieve it, even as the colleges must accept the opportunity of leadership and show that they can achieve distinction in untried and different ways.

STRUCTURAL DISTINCTIVENESS

At the level of organization, alternative college models might well show experimentation in scheduling according to the needs of particular programs, even to the extent of producing calendar variations within a university. There would be secondary benefits. It would then be impossible for comptrollers or registrars or directors of food services to go on doing things in the same old ways. The old ways would not serve the new needs. Necessity is not always the mother of invention, but it may encourage a necessary interest in change.

Could there not be more diversity in grading and evaluating processes? Certain programs might lend themselves best to letter grades, some to term letters, others to a pass-fail arrangement. Could there not also be greater use made of environmental and non-intellective variables in the student selection process? This idea has been tested at Harvard where 85 percent of two hundred young people admitted on the strength of criteria other than high college board scores graduated. In these and other ways the new colleges could help a university learn that needs vary and that procedures should be appropriate to needs.

There might also be reason to introduce variation in the social contracts that govern student life at the different colleges. Some programs might benefit by living arrangements and social regulations that would be inappropriate for another place or ethos. A pluralistic society should not be surprised by differences in its educational network—even at the levels of hours for women, dating provisions, dress regulations, drinking rules—and all of this at the same university, among its several colleges. In this, the university would be the society in microcosm. Students would get new insights into diversity and learn that privileges are sometimes commensurate with responsibilities.

Most educators today acknowledge the need for changing the quantifying mind-set that has resulted from equating course credits and unit hours with education—and the cluster colleges provide a good opportunity to break with that fixation. Let each college arrange for a unified learning experience according to the objectives and values of the college, and set appropriate graduation requirements. In some programs this might mean a prescribed set of courses; in others more freedom could be allowed, with students constructing their own programs, and the student work could be evaluated by examination. Because human abilities and interests vary, there is value in such flexibility.

Diversity in the university need not mean anarchy. There could be unifying standards. Although each college would be challenged to authenticate itself through fidelity to its own declared purposes, the quality and relevance of its work in relation to the traditional components within the system could be evaluated through all-university examinations. And other continuing kinds of comparative evaluations could be made: when students from the innovating college take courses in conventional departments in the university, when they transfer to other schools, when they enter graduate and professional programs. There would be ample opportunity to test the validity of the new by the standards of the old. Since not more than 15 percent of our institutions of higher learning show any serious inclination to innovate, the past will always be well represented.

But concern for standards is only one of the reasons given by parent organizations for insisting that off-spring colleges conform to established policies and procedures. There are also the arguments of efficiency and convenience. Large size, it is said, necessitates routinized arrangements as a safeguard to sanity. No wonder so many of us are interested in channels rather than change.

But now, in the cluster college concept, we are talking about decentralization and about dividing universities into smaller units. The concept provides an opportunity for functional individuation; further-more, computers do miracles with minutiae. We are freed by this idea and by technology to examine what the former necessity for organizational unifor-mity has done to inhibit the quest for alternative models. If the old formulas applied to the new op-portunities have a way of making over the new in the image of the old, as we suspect, and if we therefore have reason to believe that it would be better to put the new wine of innovation into new wine-skins, then we should not hesitate to challenge the supposition that colleges established within the gen-eral structure of existing universities must adhere to the organizational arrangements of the sponsoring body. Both the ends we seek and the means we need may be new ones. The principle for cluster colleges should be that the old way of doing things can always be a guideline but should never be a noose.

The issue of structural diversity in cluster colleges is raised to a new order of importance if we understand that much more than efficiency and convenience are at stake. Organizational differences—curriculum variations, social-academic interrelations, autonomy in governance—are mechanisms by which we encourage the quest of the various colleges for value commitments that will make them identifiable and intensive communities within the large and too often isomorphic university.

VALUE DISTINCTIVENESS

An educational rationale is, of course, always operative in some measure for institutions as well as individuals. Nowhere do we teach just anything; everywhere we show selectivity, taking one thing, rejecting something else. Philosophical norms, consciously or unconsciously espoused, provide the criteria for selection.

Our problem is that most schools have not been characterized by conscious effort in this area; they have not been composed of people who are what Jean-Paul Sartre called "stalkers of meaning." Consequently, the educational philosophy is often determined willy-nilly, by the pressure of external circumstances, disciplinary biases, by hoary tradition, or anticipatory opportunism. Again, on other campuses nothing is definite so nothing is definitive. Without a philosophical framework, faculty and students lack an institutional standard against which to test themselves; and this is a day when faculty need such a standard because they are at the stage of life when, as Erik Erikson put it, the issue is integrity, just as students need it because they are at the stage in life where, as Edgar Friedenberg has shown, the issue is self-identity. And neither faculty nor students can decide such issues in a void.

Too many colleges and universities are characterized by philosophical timidity or vacuity because educators have not been able to demonstrate the superiority of one educational philosophy to another, and they haven't known how to incorporate several philosophies into a given institution without fratricidal warfare. So it has seemed expedient to play down the whole business. They have decided a vacuum was better than a whirlwind.

Now we see in the concept of cluster colleges the possibility of a better solution—a solution that provides for both definition and diversity, for coteries of committed people and for challenges to all commitments.

Research findings at the Center for Research and Development in Higher Education, University of California, Berkeley, support, as mentioned earlier, what the history of education suggests; namely, that the vitality of an educational philosophy develops in direct proportion to the meanings it offers and the challenges it faces. The best educational environment is one in which there are both those who say, "We have answers," and those who say, "We have questions." Commitment benefits by criticism, for thus commitment is exercised. Criticism needs commitment; it works only in the context of real alternatives. And creativity needs both. It begins in criticism, yet, at the same time, its own validation depends on comparison. Colleges and universities, like persons, can thrive on the tensions of comparison and change if meaning can be assigned to their struggles. Men, like their muscles, go flabby in a tensionless state; but men, unlike body tissue, need meaning as well as movement for social well-being. Thus, our interest is in academic programs with distinctions that matter. Differences that make no difference, William James used to argue, are not differences.[2]

There are not many colleges in America, and almost no state universities, characterized by values so distinctive as to really shape the life of the place.

[2] James, *Pragmatism* (New York: Longmans, Green and Co., 1928), pp. 49-50.

Antioch, Reed, Goddard, Raymond, perhaps Berkeley in recent years, and a few others make contributions at this level, but the paucity of examples is proof of the conformity that underlies the alleged diversity of higher education.

And this is so at a time when Americans, moving into the epoch of automation and cybernation, are groping for goals beyond technology and for a style of life appropriate to new human and social conditions. In this context of radical change, when home and church have lost authority and values are attenuated, there is urgent need for universities to function as centers of independent thinking, committed to opening issues, probing alternatives, and yet also providing programs that stand as "life cores" in the setting of the university's impersonal, philosophically obfuscated, complex organization.

In most universities today the value vacuum at the institutional center and the near anarchy with regard to norms and models everywhere else leave the student either with no definite standard against which to test himself or only the value presuppositions of various departments—unexamined within many departments and often conflicting among departments —out of which to devise some sort of total configurational awareness. The result is an identity crisis for the institution and a disintegrative learning experience for the students.

American universities have encouraged the exploration of ideological alternatives in the classroom. We know how to keep a lot of balls in the air at the same time. But the personal commitments of the faculties and administrators have seemed so malleable or so minimal that students have often concluded that a hierarchy of values is unnecessary or impossible. But a life without distinctions is boring even as one without meaning is death. Men cannot live in a value vacuum any more than they can live in an oxygen vacuum.[3] We see this now, hence the reaction that is developing to the metaphysical inadequacies of the old liberalism and the renewed interest in an unapologetic declaration of suppositions, objectives, and norms. We are beginning again to see the ubiquity of value judgments, explicit or otherwise, even as we now concede their provisional nature.

Under the cluster college arrangement we hypothesize, the university taken as a whole would be heterogeneous, reflecting the pluralism of society. Individual colleges within the university might well be organized around, for example, a curriculum based on humanist classics, or an educational philosophy keyed to some form of essentialism or existentialism or analytic philosophy. A program centered on ur-

[3] There is in man, as Viktor Frankl has written, "the innate desire to give as much meaning as possible to one's life, to actualize as many values as possible." *The Doctor and the Soul* (New York: Alfred A. Knopf, 1960), p. x.

ban problems offered by an institution located in the city, according to the suggestion in Chapter I, or a college featuring learning by the new electronic media might be viable contributions.

The idea of cluster colleges also invites the establishment in the secular university of programs in which the great religious faiths, East and West, could speak without dilution or apology to the whole of the student's life. Traditional concepts of the separation of church and state notwithstanding, perhaps the Roman Catholic or Presbyterian churches might sponsor a college where, within the university, the Judeo-Christian teachings which have figured so prominently in our history, and still hold residual power in society, would get rigorous study.

Another college might be known for courses conceived and led by students, which cohered, say, around the study of political and social radicalism. For such a school faculty could be drawn largely from departments elsewhere in the university when needed to serve as lecturers and resource persons. This widening and recharging of the university's curriculum would mean that some of the subjects which have interested advocates of "free universities" would be studied under the aegis of accredited universities, and that some of the people now alienated because of the blandness of so many course offerings would find involvement and standing in established schools.

Students in universities featuring value-oriented cluster colleges would be able to choose among colleges, each having a special character. Participants in these small schools would be members of a community, in fellowship with those who have made commitments and exercised self-discipline in order to achieve goals that would not otherwise be possible. Yet they would be members also of a large, diversified university.

The student's experiences in the new college would differ from those he would encounter if he studied one or another specialization in this or that department of a more conventional institution. The value commitments of a cluster college would give it institutional character and, since most of a student's work would be done in one college, a large part of his program would be imbued with the educational and social priorities of the school's philosophy of education.

Furthermore, the residential aspect of the cluster college plan provides an opportunity to establish a climate of learning that can carry the values of the program to the student at many levels. Much of a student's learning takes place outside the classroom through various informal encounters. Thus, a college of consequence will offer its students both standards and community.

Community is not possible without standards. And

while standards can be imposed without community, they are more easily achieved where community exists. When the educational system does not provide them, the young lapse into apathy or opt for anarchy.

Value-oriented cluster colleges would not exist in isolation, and the perspectives of each program would not go unchallenged. Students would take some courses elsewhere in the university; faculties would have full standing in the larger organization; the diversity of the university would provide options and correctives to the stance of any one college. These would not be cloistered colleges, but the philosophy and structure of each program would be pointed toward making student and faculty learning experiences deeply personal.

Some educators think that making education personal means the creation of a protective society where faculty brood over students as God brooded over his creation. This is oppressive personalization. Others think it is just a matter of mix, or of arranging tracks that bring people into physical proximity to the extent that they are obliged to greet each other as they pass. This is the grunt-as-you-bump approach, and one capable of achieving only perfunctory personalization. But there is a vastly different sense in which education can be personal, and to understand it we should read Martin Buber's essays entitled "Education" and "The Education of Character." There he talks about "inclusion," about getting into a human relationship in which you truly "experience the other side." Buber illustrates: "A man belabours another, who remains quite still. Then let us assume that the striker suddenly receives in his soul the blow which he strikes. . . . . For the space of a moment he experiences the situation from the other side." [4] How many of us think about making education personal in this inclusive sense? Hear Buber again:

A man caresses a woman, who lets herself be caressed. Then let us assume that he feels the contact from two sides—with the palm of his hand still, but also with the woman's skin too. The two-fold nature of the gesture, as one that takes place between two persons, thrills through the depth of enjoyment in his heart and stirs it. [5]

Buber's last illustration had better be given a metaphorical rather than a literal application. Yet the image of the caress is helpful in showing that it is possible, not regularly but occasionally, to extend a relationship to the level where "the other person becomes present . . . for all time." Most of us know little of such dialogical relationships. In cluster colleges, however, under the terms I have sketched, students and faculty together would be encouraged to achieve it because they would be obliged to ask, "What

[4] Buber, *Between Man and Man* (Boston: Beacon Press, 1955), p. 96.
[5] *Ibid.*

has meaning for me and what has importance for others?" "How do we develop an ethic of individual honesty and an ethic of social responsibility?" Confronted by the university's diversity, its pluralism and anarchy, they would ask, "What is the basis for authority?" "What do we hold in common?" There are no questions more relevant for our time.

Are we willing to run the risks of substantive diversity? It could mean a radical change for the public university in its relationship to society. If the pressures of constituencies can force private institutions, the "independent" colleges, into an uncritical acceptance of what are thought to be societal norms, it may be even more difficult to establish divergent value options in public universities. Embodying a "service concept" and required to live by the sort of consensus that is necessary to secure a broad base of support, these schools are almost totally mimetic in values. And we seem to prefer it that way.

The problems, of course, would not all be external; there is also the threat of schism within. American institutions of higher learning, despite their historical perspective, scholarly acumen, and collective erudition, may not be sophisticated enough to encourage diversity on basic issues without incurring destructive consequences.

Even if a modest beginning were made, with emphasis put first on structural distinctiveness, allowing idealogical distinctiveness to emerge later, as much trouble would be generated from within as from without. Assuming that governing boards were willing to grant autonomy to the cluster colleges, autonomy would not, of course, guarantee innovation. If leaders of the new programs have the same hierarchy of values as those on the old campuses, they will talk of distinctiveness but strive for parity. New colleges may, therefore, project the idea of distinctiveness only as a means for establishing their identity and their budgets, with their eye on the ultimate end of matching their progenitors in size, research, and those other "distinctions" that have recently come under justifiable criticism. Success is measured by standards and, remember, standards are fixed by values. Can the new programs be significantly different if their leadership measures achievement by the old values? Our faith is that *hubris* does yield to the power of a higher affection, as religions have shown; and therefore we may hope that both organizational change and ideological identity will triumph in the cluster colleges.

Clark Kerr has decided that the most serious crisis in higher education is in undergraduate training, particularly of students in general education and those not yet ready to declare a specialization.[6] Roger Heyns of Berkeley has argued that lack of agreement

---

[6] Kerr, *Center Diary: 14*, October-November, 1966 (Santa Barbara: Center for the Study of Democratic Institutions), p. 11.

on the nature of the university is perhaps our most serious problem.[7] Cluster colleges conceived as alternative models to the dominant learning environment are a means of getting at both issues. Such colleges can yield fruitful responses to these challenges if they are granted sufficient freedom to establish curricula, facilities, and procedures distinguished by the values they have made their own.

This is a way to help youth develop a capacity for judgment, give essence as well as form to the diversity of American higher education, and bring meaning to the experiences of all participants.

[7] Heyns, "The Nature of the Academic Community," speech before American Council of Education, New Orleans, October 13, 1966.

IV

THE PROBLEMS
OF SIZE: SMALL SIZE

It is provided in the essence of things that from any
fruition of success, no matter what, shall come forth something to make a greater struggle necessary.
—Walt Whitman

At this time, when the attractions of the small
college are being offered as the answer to the problem
of large size, it is essential to recognize that the problems of smallness rival the problems of bigness. We
need to know not only what we are getting away from
but also what we are getting into. Like the boy who
leaves the big family and the large house to start a
little family and live in a small apartment, only to
find his responsibilities extended by that contraction,
the small college breeds new problems by solving old
ones. Indeed, to make education personal, to assume
responsibility for the environment, to claim a separ-

ate but equal status, poses problems of awesome proportions.

To make education personal is to take on a concern for the whole person. The ramifications of such a value commitment are profound. Recall, for example, the extent to which such an emphasis challenges the adequacy of the departmental structure of the typical college, in which the student's mind is either divided up among the departments or encapsulated within one. Furthermore, when the momentum of the truly responsive student, which carries the learning encounter far beyond the borders of any circumscribed field, is joined with the cross-disciplinary and integrative configurations emerging through the new media —developments of special interest to the new colleges —one can see the extent to which the subject-matter disciplines are threatened by cluster college proposals.

Again, when education is personal, the concern is not only for the student as he is but also for what he can become. Education, as Buber has written, is "education for character" whenever the student is taught not just something but something important.[1] The values of the faculty member become involved in the determination of what is "important," and what the professor declares important may be expected to affect the values of the student. The cluster

[1] Buber, *Between Man and Man*, p. 104.

college concept, emphasizing the response of the total person to the whole of life, requires that considerable attention be given to one's educational objectives and value judgments. Most faculty members, however, do not like to have their deepest assumptions challenged, and they prefer tasks that focus on the informational rather than on the formational.

When the student is accepted as a person as well as a student, he expects to know the professor as a person as well as a scholar. Academic dramaturgy has its place, but in education that is personal the professor must drop his mask and face his students undisguised. He can do this without loss of dignity, but not without the revelation of preconceptions, attitudes, and personal goals; it is the risk the faculty takes when it agrees to the total educational involvement promised in the cluster college concept.

The emphasis on the individual in the learning situation provides incentive and participation for the student, but it also provides a set of psychosocial problems. Because the student's views are considered important, he sometimes concludes that everything he says is important. Or, since the interior life of the student is presented as the other side of his exterior performance—and both, he is told, are important in the expression of the "total person"—the temptation is strong for him to give snap responses rather than disciplined answers, especially when he has not studied the night before class. Many a seminar has been killed by a blatherskite.

Students in large, impersonal institutions may view the faculty with awe or indifference because of distance. But in a cluster college distance is gone, and familiarity has been known, at least sometimes, to breed contempt. Education elsewhere may be impersonal and students powerless, but for cluster college students the problems are different: they arise as the result of too many personal contacts and too much involvement. Faculty members are especially vulnerable to the pressure produced by the closeness. Students made heady by excessive attention may show small respect for faculty authority and professional competence. Word gets around fast in a small student body, and criticism of faculty members may become canonical without being inspired.

Not only the professors, but the program of a whole college can be damaged in these ways. As David Riesman puts it, "Student complaint is everywhere a censor of reform, for the students have the power by nonattendance and resistance to scuttle new enterprises before they are fully launched." [2]

Some cluster college students, out of shyness and self-consciousness or perhaps dullness, do not take advantage of the arrangements for intellectual discus-

[2] Riesman, "Notes on New Universities: British and American," *Universities Quarterly,* March, 1966, p. 144.

sions with faculty. Although they may eat in the same hall as do faculty and could arrange to sit with them, they avoid such encounters. They find they have nothing to say, or they get tired of academic topics and prefer small talk with their peer group. After all, adults over thirty. . .

Again, while all colleges and universities emphasize the need for criticism of social values, the cluster colleges so intensify issues and relations that a large percentage of their students become active critics of the standards and tastes of society. Criticism may be what the society needs, and this is an argument in support of cluster colleges; but it must also be acknowledged that the students who reject the achievement-oriented culture often find their political and social circles more and more constricted. Their estrangement can end in anomie—the social vacuum created by the absence of shared norms and values. They put themselves in a position, then, where they must find something to fill the void.

Some students attempt to fill it by forming a coterie of the "elect." Like the despised and rejected minorities in the early Christian era, they band together to await the eventual repudiation of their foes by the forces of history. Meanwhile, they revel in their suffering, scorn as sinful any effort to achieve a *rapprochement* with "corrupt" institutions, and find their entertainment in the foibles of others or the improvisation of their own "in-group" humor.

Some fill the void by personal introversion. They follow up the college's commitment to social and political analysis and the concomitant sensitivity to human relations with a probing, relentless introspection that peels off the layers of the human psyche until it is raw and bleeding or until nothing is left. To be sure, this inclination to introspection is not limited to students of the cluster colleges. But it is fair to point out that these schools activate an unparalleled degree of individual introversion by their emphasis on individual involvement, by their preference for facilities that tend to result in "cloistered colleges" (or ghettos) that threaten to close in the open spaces and turn the activities of mind and body inward, and by the fact that they are for the most part recently established colleges which, like infants in their self-conscious newness, keep touching themselves to confirm their existence.

Now if students focus attention on human beings and human beings fail them, if they look to their own resources but find only emptiness, their disenchantment often results in bitterness. At that point either they separate themselves from the source of their trouble, the college, or they develop a feeling of futility sufficient to paralyze creativity, vitiate commitment, and produce mediocrity and apathy. One of the strengths of an experimental cluster college is that it will tolerate almost anything but indifference. This being the case, if a student cannot make some sort of commitment and keep up the pace, he may choose hostility as the alternative to indifference. Thus many students leave the cluster college or, if they stay, retreat into various private pursuits. As a consequence, the community becomes fragmented; and it is on the success of community that so much depends.

Even those students who remain in college—for the most part happily—chafe under the absence of privacy, which is another by-product of the enforced closeness of the cluster college arrangement. Students complain of being together so much that they come to anticipate everyone's response to every situation. While some surely profit by this kind of contact, others become hard or detached as a way of protecting their inner freedom. Still others melt and, by losing their identity, lose what the college was meant to establish. Faculty members may complain not only that their contacts with students are time-consuming, but worse, that they themselves feel overcome by psychic fatigue. So the professors who thought it would be stimulating to "live in" decide that in the interest of maintaining perspective they will move off campus. And the students decide that the legitimate claims of privacy dictate an apartment somewhere away from campus rules and the college's high level of expectation. While the cluster college has many advantages, provision for privacy is not one of them. Ironically, a student may choose such a college for the very features—participation, sharing, involvement—which in time make him decide that what he really wants is to be alone.

Cluster colleges have been set up as residential programs because it seemed important to keep the student, as we say, in the climate of learning. A large part, perhaps most, of a student's learning takes place outside the classroom. Therefore, in the interests of enriching and accelerating the learning process, the colleges surround him with out-of-class personalities and activities. But within the last several years students have increasingly rejected the residential college culture and shown a preference for small, informal, private living arrangements that cannot be reconciled either with the structured high-rise dormitory life in the large university or with the open environment of the small residential college. The one lacks character, the other privacy.

Pressure is already building up in the established cluster colleges to allow more off-campus housing. But will this movement end in a return to the brief-case faculty and the scattered student body? And what will the interest in anonymity mean for the goal of community within a college? If the cluster colleges opt for both the residential and off-campus housing arrangements, as some are doing, how will they avoid that two-culture division—the "townies" versus the "living-in" groups—that has so often plagued the traditional schools? How can cluster colleges establish community, which calls for self-discipline and social responsibility, and also provide for independence and its variant, privacy? This situation presents itself for solution at a time when the alienation of students from so much of modern institutional life is driving them to the extremes of apathy, which emasculates the spirit of independence, or to anarchy, which makes community impossible.

As for the cluster college emphasis on institutional autonomy, there are evident advantages in introducing change into an established university by bringing new and different components into a federated grouping. But the special arrangements, exemptions, and accommodations necessitated by the establishment of such colleges within the context of an established university have an astonishingly large number of effects.

Although the faculty members of the new college work harder because they carry the weight of proof, they also develop feelings of insecurity when they learn that those who try to lead must go it alone. Their professional standing is threatened, not only because they are usually involved in work that takes them outside their field of specialization, but also because they learn that by daring to be different they are risking the disapproval of their peers. And this is so in a day when a man's standing with his guild is likely to mean more to him than his standing with his college.

If the faculty member of a cluster college, because of his direct and extended involvement with students, is permitted an adjustment in his teaching load, committee assignments, or other responsibilities, his colleagues elsewhere in the university are likely to complain that he is being given preferential treatment. On the other hand, if he is held to the conventional standards for advancement, usually weighted on the side of research and publication, he cannot long give himself to students or conform to the ideals that brought the college into being. It is this pressure that finally makes the faculty of an innovating college responsive to proposals for returning to established work patterns, familiar arrangements, and the tracks of habit and tradition. And this is why the life span of radically experimental programs has been about seven years, and why an innovative college is not likely to be again so radical as on the day it opens. The threat of a short life, or an increasingly conforming one, is only slightly mitigated by the fact that the cluster college is organized in the context of an established university which presumably has a vested interest in the survival and effectiveness of one of its own enterprises.

How generous everyone is toward the idea of an innovating college within a university until that college turns out to be truly different. It was to this point that Machiavelli spoke, albeit within the context of his own world:

It should be borne in mind that there is nothing more difficult to arrange, more doubtful of success, and more dangerous to carry through than initiating changes in a state's constitution. The innovator makes enemies of all those who prospered under the old order, and only lukewarm support is forthcoming from those who would prosper under the new.[3]

An innovative college, characterized not only by openness to change but also by the vitality of high purpose, stands as a critical conscience to the status quo. It is not surprising, then, that the attempts to isolate or crush the upstart begin fairly soon. Those who live by habit call for order. Those who handle volume demand routine. Those who work with the public want harmony. The effect of the resultant pressures on the students of the cluster college is as profound as it is on their teachers and administrators. The spirit of youth may impel the students to rally to the cause, but they can then invest so much of their time and emotional capital in the life of the college that they

[3] Machiavelli, *The Prince*, trans. by Ninian Hill Thomson (Oxford: Clarendon Press, 1938), pp. 34-35.

have nothing left for the interests of the university and the outside world. They become isolated and provincial. Students from other programs in the university stay away from them. Centripetal forces take over within the college while the university succumbs to centrifugal ones.

Students in any college that is new or small or experimental will be racked with uncertainties. Have they made the right choice? Is it worth the fight? What does the future hold? These are old questions, but in a cluster college everything seems magnified, intensified, individualized. Environments are never passive wrappings into which we put our meanings; as McLuhan has emphasized, they have a meaning of their own and a vital effect on us.

The new demands of the new schools sometimes confuse issues for top-level administrators too—even those well oriented to the goals of the cluster college. Must every innovation in the experimental college have its equivalent arrangement in the other components of the university? Should the faculty of the new college, for example, get new facilities while the faithful old guard continue to work in outmoded quarters? New facilities may be needed to achieve the goals of the innovative curriculum, but of course the traditional program could profit by new facilities, too. Must there be uniform social regulations for students across the university? The cluster college program, in which students and faculty are together in a variety of situations, results in an informality of dress and personal style not only different from but probably offensive to conventionally oriented elements in the university. Such differences produce rich diversity; but one man's diversity is another man's damnation.

Now, if these are the problems that attach to the characteristic features of the cluster college program, what can be done to save the good and make tolerable the bad? The cluster colleges hold tremendous potential for good. They bring flexibility to universities with stiff joints; they are a means whereby universities can retain the advantages of smallness while growing large; they are a mechanism for experimentation in an epoch of revolutionary change.

The principle behind the goal of active involvement for the student in the learning experience is sound, and the achievement of the goal is worth the struggle. Numerous studies show that when students are given responsibility and become personally involved in their work, they learn faster and better. The student's participation in the life of the university can be enriched, and his isolation in the small college reduced, by bringing in and rotating students and professors from other colleges in the university, and also visitors from the outside. It could be made mandatory that the cluster college student take a portion of his work elsewhere. Study in other programs of the university, or in another state or country, should have a broadening effect and help to reduce subjectivity and provincialism.

Professors involved in cluster college experimentation must be compensated properly for their labors. The hours and energy required for the close student-faculty relations should be recognized and appropriate adjustments made. University administrators can show by the rewards and sanctions they establish that they are serious about innovation. Change, like excellence, comes at a high price. Priorities must be set in such a way that there can be no question about the authority and dignity of those participating in the new programs.

Because having students in residence seems crucial to the purposes of a cluster college, it is important to arrange housing for the students and faculty so as to provide both companionship and privacy. Single rooms, sitting room-bedroom combinations, outside stairways, and other architectural provisions safeguard privacy without the loss of the "living-learning," student-faculty contacts. Good construction reduces noise to tolerable levels. Carpeting is economically feasible as well as aesthetically pleasing. Perhaps it would be desirable to have suites of rooms opening on a shared lounge for freshmen, and rooms with doors opening to the outside, or at least to outside corridors, for upperclassmen, who could fix their own hours. The college governing body could set interhouse visiting hours. A sitting room–bedroom combination allows for entertaining and privacy. If costs are too high for such construction, it might be better to have all students living in the surrounding neighborhood and coming together for certain meals and programs, in addition to following their regular on-campus class schedules. This arrangement would be preferable to the huge dormitories into which students are at present herded.

Students who study hard, especially if they are required to live in conventional dormitories, must get out of their cellblocks and find renewal for body and spirit in physical exercise, cultural events, and travel. Otherwise they atrophy. The English concept of "sauntering and sprinting" is sound; it suggests that there is a time for hard and rigorous study and a time for play and adventure. Students will achieve this balance only if the college makes it clear that its hierarchy of values includes sauntering as well as sprinting.

There must be at least provisional autonomy for the cluster colleges if they are to be innovative. Each new college should be granted the freedom to declare its objectives and organize itself accordingly. Thus, the college will have character, and the students enrolled in it will learn the meaning of choice in the context of diversity.[4] The college may be homogeneous, but the university—a federated system of different styles, philosophies, and programs—will be heterogeneous. The educational autonomy of the cluster college should be limited only by the need to avoid unnecessary duplication of services and facilities. Obviously, determining the perimeter of autonomy calls for judgments and decisions that must be worked out in the crucible of experience. But all limitations on autonomy should be tested against the university's commitment to institutionalize change.

The problems which derive from the cluster college concept are manifold. We must be mindful always, as we move to compensate for the problems of large universities in American higher education, that the problems of small-sized colleges will not be small. However, we should proceed in the knowledge that every significant change gives rise to a new set of contingencies, and that achievements to which these changes may lead transcend the problems.

---

[4] In his book *Changing Values in College: An Exploratory Study of the Impact of College Teaching* (New York: Harper & Row, 1958) Philip E. Jacob argued that most colleges and universities have little effect on student values. Where there is institutional distinctiveness and values are emphasized, however, students are affected.

V

AN ALTERNATIVE MODEL OF INCLUSIVE INSTITUTIONAL GOVERNANCE

Education for the whole man in a world culture—that is the paradigm, I believe, for "the next historic transformation of man." The end sought in education for the whole man is what the Greeks called *aretê*, the total excellence of the person. The role of a world culture is *paideia*, the Greek concept emphasizing the utilization of all facets of life in the achievement of human excellence, although now that concept is to be extended to include the world. However, nothing less than radical reforms in institutional arrangements will suffice if education in a technological age is to resist present tendencies toward specialism and depersonalization and emphasize instead the development of unified man in international perspective.

Resources for such comprehensive reformation are,

in fact, available in the prevailing model—the "versity"—but, because we cannot posit with confidence the superiority of any one plan of reform, the better strategy for finally attaining substantial change is to introduce alternative models that will provide diverse approaches to the future. The cluster college concept, in my opinion, is the best mechanism for achieving what is needed. Diversity in educational philosophies, objectives, values, in curricula, programs, procedures, in facilities and environments would provide bases for comparison. Also, the resultant atmosphere of openness would encourage creativity and help to overcome the present paucity of radical, as opposed to instrumental, ideas. Perhaps most important would be the actualization of an achievement we have long claimed; that is, an educational system in which the full range of individual abilities and human interests can be served and developed to their fullest. The dominance of professionally oriented faculties and a consensus mentality on campus make such a claim at present farcical.

Perhaps there would be value, with reference to the imperatives and constraints to change, in viewing a particular area of university life where reforms are needed and in considering in some detail an alternative model that seems feasible.

One area of concern these days is that of institutional governance, and the alternative model that will be described is a variation of the well-known "academic community" concept but, in this case, with variations sufficient to make a difference in kind, not degree. This idea for change will be applied to universities instead of colleges because the problems in complex universities seem especially vexing. But the points of emphasis have transfer value for colleges and may indeed be more easily realized in them.

A further reason for taking up the matter of governance and the prospects for innovation at that level is because administrators have gained a reputation in recent years as the friends of change, especially as compared to faculty. They have had it too good. It is true that most curricular experimentation today has been initiated by administrators and that faculty have not been disposed to reform themselves. But every interest group on campus can be persuaded to tolerate innovation—elsewhere. Students are responsive to reforms for the institution, but less so toward those that would change individuals. Faculty urge administrators to show courage in liberalizing parietal rules for students, but they resist administrative "interference" in academic programs. Administrators promote experimentation in the curriculum but show no particular audacity about changes in the administrative organization chart by which they derive their authority and security. No, we are all in this thing together, and that is why the model of the university as community may be a better option for the future than the present hierarchical form of institutional governance.

As noted earlier, it is the view of Roger Heyns, Chancellor of the University of California, Berkeley, that there is now no agreement on the basic nature of the academic community. Furthermore, says Heyns, "our lack of clarity, our lack of agreement as to the essential properties of the academic life has made us indecisive, uncertain and divided." [1]

It is obvious that the modern university is divided. That it is indecisive because it is uncertain about its essential nature is open to question. Is there not, in fact, general agreement, both inside and outside academe, that the university is essentially a center of service? Its service, to be sure, takes many forms and means many things, but everything it does is a form of service. Thus it is not enough to define the university as a center of learning, as Chancellor Heyns would have it be, although providing the setting for learning and encouraging the activity of learning are important university services. Nor is it just a center of teaching, although teaching is still one prime service. (But not so important as many academics think. One of two great delusions, according to Henry Steele Commager, is that "everything must be *taught*, in-

---

[1] Heyns, "The Nature of the Academic Community."

stead of learned." [2]) Above all else the university offers services; this is the key to its nature.

Division comes, then, not over the basic nature of the university but over what forms its service shall take, and with what priorities. This lack of agreement divides the university and makes it indecisive.

Some people, largely off campus, want the university's service to be judged by how well it perpetuates the past. Others, more on campus than off, want the university to emphasize the future, to act as a center of independent thinking characterized by a capacity for innovation. There are those who want the university to emphasize training for the professions; professional service, they argue, should dominate over, say, the liberal arts. There is an expanding minority of students who want the university to be an agent of direct social action. Professors, for their part, usually want the university to provide the locus for scholarly research and the amenities of the civilized life.

ESTABLISHING A HIERARCHY OF SERVICE

The essential question, in the midst of rival expectations, is this: Is there a way by which the various

[2] Henry Steele Commager, R. W. McEwen, and B. Blanchard, *Education in a Free Society*, II (Pittsburgh: University of Pittsburgh, 1960), 14. The other delusion is that *everything* must be taught. "We seem to think that because all knowledge is the province of the scholar, every university must take all knowledge as its province."

interpretations of the university's work can be adjudicated and a hierarchy of services established? There is: by giving a new twist to the concept of the university as an academic community and redefining it to mean a community of students, faculty, and administrators—a tripartite community with each section having a vital role in policy formulation, in the defense of the university's integrity, and in setting the limits of service.

Such a community cannot begin to take shape until the participants agree at least provisionally on key assumptions, goals, and values. Individuals and institutions live by certitudes that give meaning to their activities, and community is not possible until we know what those values are. One trouble with the concept of the university as a center of learning, as advocated by Chancellor Heyns, is the implicit assumption that such a center is nonjudgmental and open to all perspectives. Yet what a university is willing to learn is affected by what it is looking for. The Chancellor is among those saying that "the university is not an instrument of direct social action," and also that it "embraces and exalts the reasoned, examined life." [3] To students of the radical left on the Berkeley campus, however, the reasoned and examined life reveals that the University of California is very much

---

[3] Heyns, "The Nature of the Academic Community."

an instrument of direct social action—one of those instruments that serve the interests of the system. Obviously the value perspectives of the chancellor and those of his protagonists influence their divergent conclusions. It is always so.

But can the modern academic community ever "define" itself, even provisionally? Does not the illustration just given show the sort of division that makes a "communiversity" impossible? Community requires a measure of agreement on norms and attitudes. What hope is there for that?

THE FALLACY OF SOCIETAL DEPENDENCY

There is no hope if the university's values are to be set by the societal context. Ours is a pluralistic society containing atheists and fundamentalists, radicals and reactionaries. It is heterogeneous, including every gradation of economic and intellectual sophistication. In earlier times there seemed to be an operational social consensus—albeit amid claims to diversity—a "public mind," especially in regard to ethical values for youth. The home and church, as centers of moral influence, gave that consensus vitality. But today those former authority agents have declined in influence, and what leadership we have comes from the nation-state. It is leadership by default, not design. The agencies of government in a democracy are commissioned to implement more than innovate, sustain more than create, and provide structure once the way is known. Leadership from Washington in the realm of values is especially difficult. The nation-state must fall back on whatever consensus there is at the level of the lowest common societal denominator. At a time when values have become individualistic, as today, not much substance remains for group convictions. No wonder the university is divided and indecisive. It is still trying to follow, but there is no leader.

One reason why the concept of *in loco parentis* is doomed on most campuses is that it is now impossible for officials to stand in the place of parents regarding the student's personal and social life because there is no longer any effective agreement among parents as to what the university is to stand for. On all the controversial issues—alcohol and other drugs, hours for women and interdorm visits between the sexes, contraceptive information and "the pill"—administrators cannot hope to be guided by a nonexistent parental consensus.

However, are the prospects of finding the essentials for community any better within the institution of higher learning? The modern university, many believe, is a log-rolling anarchy within which various interest groups—faculty, students, administrators, alumni—work out compromises and accommodations at points of contact in order to be left free to invest most of their time in various forms of privatism. As one writer has put it: "In the absence of some concept of the mission of the university, these matters are decided in response to the individual ambitions and convenience of professors, to outside pressures, or to departmental imperialism furthered by a species of interdepartmental log-rolling." [4] This problem is compounded at Berkeley and a few other places by a movement, involving students and nonstudents, away from community and toward the creation of a militant subdivision powerful enough to play the game of confrontation politics, including the strategy of strike.

What chance have we for community in the university if there is no semblance of unity there?

BASES FOR COOPERATION

I believe that, despite divergencies, the various groups in academe still have enough in common to provide the basis for meaningful community, and that it can be achieved without the sacrifice of diversity.

We begin with the fact, generally accepted if broadly defined, that the university is a center of service. And if leadership as to the kinds, quality, and purposes of that service cannot be expected from the

[4] René de Williamson, "Church and University," *Faculty Forum*, March, 1966, p. 1.

culture of a society in conflict, then we may take it as a second point of agreement that the university must become a center of service as delimited by the academic community itself. The concept of service is not to be lost but found by being defined.

Now, it has already been argued that the university's demarcation of services will depend on the values of its community. But does this community hold anything in common? The answer is *yes*.

The academic community shares belief in the necessity for order—the order of time, place, and manner. Our work, whatever its form, cannot proceed without regard for this essential. It is a community, furthermore, that believes in the life of the mind, in the "reasoned and examined life." To surrender this is to yield the right to rational criticism. And criticism is essential for finite man, the imperfect being who tends to absolutize himself. But we also acknowledge the merit in anarchy—that is, order jarred and rearranged—because we believe in the emotions, in the life of the spirit. To reason is not necessarily to be right; often reasons are emotions rationalized. Furthermore, as the mind fosters criticism the emotions encourage creativity—another need of finite man, the partial being who yearns for completeness. The academic community emphasizes the life of the spirit, even to the extreme of anarchy. We also believe in the necessity of order but with the

117

option of anarchy—that is, of order individualized.

Thus, another commitment is to the individual, creature of mind and spirit, and to the quest of the individual for an ethic of personal honesty. The other side of this coin is the belief in the necessity of society (the milieu for community) and the need for an ethic of social responsibility. Yet the ethic of social responsibility is built on the ethic of personal honesty. If the academic community is to err, it elects to do so on the side of individualism.

We believe in the necessity for value judgments, and we make them, as the preceding priorities illustrate. But we are human and we live in a secular community devoid of divine revelation. Without denying the possibility of such revelation, we assert that those who claim it cannot agree on what has been revealed, nor on its meaning for the public life. Therefore, we acknowledge the provisional nature of all value judgments. To stand for something gives us a basis for character and action. To admit its provisional nature encourages humility and an openness to change.

FREEDOM AND RESTRAINT

Are not the restraints imposed on this concept of community, some will say, likely to be unacceptable to those who take individual freedom as their ideal?

May not the call to community be but another way for the Establishment to control individuals and effect order on its own terms? Community encourages conformity.

This threat is real, but it can be mitigated by defining community as an arrangement whereby individuals come together, voluntarily imposing certain limitations on themselves in order to achieve ends which fulfill them in ways not otherwise possible. In the society at large, limitations on the individual are externally imposed by law and order. In the family, perimeters are set by filial duty. But in the community of which I speak, the limitations are more nearly self-imposed; the fellowship is voluntary, the assent personal, the commitments entered into freely. Community, to be sure, is built on ideology and discipline. Both are essential but neither need be coercive.

To this must be added the point of the existentialists; men either consciously take a stand for certain values or are, in fact, subject to the values of the status quo and the control of some purposeful faction. It is popular now for alienated youth, refusing to be subjects of the system, to say that they are "opting out"—implying a determination to stand free of value judgments. Actually, theirs is an unlikely achievement. Not many opt out—only the suicides. The rest move from something to something, from system to schism, from Establishment to disestablishmen-

119

tarianism, from theme to improvisation. Life, after all, is a matter of taking a stance.

The college as community has the greatest potential benefit for those whose stance is individualism because perhaps no other arrangement so emphasizes the validity of both order and anarchy, mind and spirit, the ethic of social responsibility transcended only by the ethic of personal honesty. This is a community open to individuals determined to transcend it.

Young people need to belong to such a fellowship precisely because the task of adolescence is self-identification, and with the anxiety of their uncertainty they need both the security of a purposeful entity and something against which to test their efforts at independence. Yet the relationship is transactional. Their restless strivings contribute to the vitality and integrity of the community they challenge.

THE STRUCTURE OF THE NEW COMMUNITY

That which the academic community believes about man and history, about the individual in relation to the group, about how we learn and what it means, will serve as the university's ideological foundation. (Do not speak of "the end of ideology." Ideology changes; it may mean "process," but it never ends.) However, while we must establish our ideology or philosophy of education—and in a time of philosophical timidity it is a contribution for an institution to be consciously at work in this area—yet we must also press beyond ideals and attitudes to organizational arrangements that will be instruments for achieving community. Otherwise, disaster is assured at the point where ideals must be interpreted according to the needs of specific situations. This is the problem religions always confront. Everyone is in favor of justice, love, and the other tenets of religion. It is in the applications of these abstract principles to hard realities that difficulties arise.

How, then, should the university be organized so as to bring into practice the ideals of community? Here is one model.

All of us must live with the reality that universities are increasingly large and complex organizations. Many of us live in such settings. Yet, as Max Lerner has emphasized, it is important for the individual to relate to a group small enough for it to be affected by his presence even as it affects him, and we ought therefore to provide "the small organic group as the life-core, even while we are a part of the big organization." [5]

[5] Lerner, "The Revolutionary Frame of Our Time," in *The College and the Student*, L. E. Dennis and J. D. Kauffman, eds. (Washington: American Council on Education, 1966), p. 16.

The structuring of the university into undergraduate colleges, as in the cluster college plan, is the best way to achieve such a life-core. Each college should have not more than five hundred to eight hundred students, because it is impossible for the average faculty member or student to establish his presence in a larger setting. A good rule of thumb is this: if the faculty is too large for members to know each other by name, there may be no name-calling but neither will there be much personal involvement. And in these colleges education is to be personal.

Each college should have sufficient autonomy to establish its own curriculum and special character. As for governance, a college council with membership drawn from faculty, administrators, and students would provide leadership for policies and practices therein. Yet there must be university-wide objectives and standards, and they should be set by a university council, the highest policy body in the institution. The membership of this committee would include the university president (in the University of California and other large systems, each campus may be regarded as a university, and this member would be the chancellor); the financial vice-president (or vice-chancellor); the academic vice-president (or vice-chancellor); the provosts of the several colleges; and an appropriate number of faculty, students—including graduate students—and general constituency representatives.

The number drawn from faculty, students, and constituency would vary with the size of the university. But certain guidelines can be set down for the determination of the size and character of the university council. First, the council must be small enough to assure direct and informal discussion. Second, it must have power, dignity, and diversity in representation. This is the answer to the question, "Can any good thing come out of a committee?" Seldom do we get out of anything more than we put into it. Third, most student members should be elected to this body after having had experience on a college council. Fourth, constituency representatives should be elected from what may be called the constituency committee, a group with advisory power that replaces the traditional board of trustees. Constituency representatives would be voting members of the university council. Fifth, the articles of incorporation and university legal documents would be in the names of a consortium of university council members drawn from those of legal age. They would compose the "legal entity." Sixth, the tripartite concept should apply to the council in that one third of the membership would be from administration (perhaps including staff as well as constituency representatives), another third from the faculties of the colleges, and the final third from the various college student bodies. The size of the university and the number of persons in general administration would determine whether provosts would be grouped with administration or faculty. All university administrators would be accountable to the university council. An executive committee of the council would see to the implementation of council policies.

The president of the university might well be chosen from the provosts on the council and serve a four-year, renewable term. Thus he would come to the presidency with faculty and administrative experience as dictated by his earlier participation on a college council. His term in office would be long enough to draw out creativity but not long enough to harden mistakes. And any administrative "honors" would be viewed in the context of his eventual return to the faculty.

Just as the university is to be organized by colleges, yet with provision for the university's cohesiveness, so each college should be organized on a collegial plan. Within the last fifty years in American higher education, authority for academic programs has shifted. First delegated from the board of trustees to the president, it was later transferred to the deans, and now to faculty. Some fear that the next step is for control to be given over to students. But there is a better option.

The great majority of American students are not eager to "take over" the university, but they are concerned to be involved in all aspects of its life. Likewise, in recent times administrators have been considered by some faculties to be at best second-class citizens and at worst toadies of the trustees. But if the essential nature of the academic community is service— and that means service to the needs of all members within the community as well as service to society at large—then the better option would be to have policy for the college set by the college council, composed of faculty, students, and administration and including constituency representatives who would bring to the college as well as to the university the needs, interests, perspectives, and criticisms from the societal situation. Thus each college would have all its components represented at the highest level of policy formulation and would have a mechanism for making the college sensitive to, though no longer at the mercy of, the culture within which it operates.

This model of community government, a variation of which has been tested at Antioch College but not in any major university, offers a viable alternative both to prevailing bureaucratic arrangements which foster conservatism by favoring hierarchical authority, and to proposed organizational revisions as offered by a few student extremists, which would result in *co-gobierno*—co-government by students and faculty alone. Furthermore, the prospects for true community in the university would be enhanced by having all interest groups represented in a calibrated fashion on the university council and the college councils.

LEADERSHIP CIRCUITS

In a day when the old static intellectual structure in the university, with its compartmentalization of knowledge and specializations, is giving way, and the challenge is to live with probability, contingency, and flexible configurations, a kindred development in administration and another feature of this alternative model would be the establishment of job circuits that would break the inertia and defensiveness that tend to exist where fixed responsibilities and long-term, isolated assignments predominate. Now that computers and office technicians are available to handle routine work and assure procedural continuity, rotating administrative personnel around a circuit of offices would improve prospects for fresh ideas and the continuing analysis of established arrangements.

How could this be done? If the university were organized on the collegium plan, then it could be arranged for the faculty within each college to elect certain of its members to pursue two administrative circuits. One would lead selected personnel out of the faculty, in sequence, into the dean of students' office for a two-year stint and then on into the provost's chair for another two-year term before returning them to the faculty. The other circuit would put selected faculty members, in sequence, first as head of the registrar's office and then in charge of the admissions office before returning them to the faculty. Only the financial officer of the college—the bursar, English-style—would be a stationary employee, plus the clerks, secretaries, and technicians of particular offices. By this arrangement, members of the faculty would learn the administrative side of things and would operate as policy makers. And hopefully the titles would sit lightly on their heads.

These four administrative officers, plus four full-time faculty members, four students (perhaps one sophomore, two juniors, one senior), and the bursar would comprise each college council, that body making general policy for the college. In addition, the faculty of each college could have its meetings and committees, as could the students. Campus social life should be based in the colleges and put largely in the hands of those living there.

ASSUMPTIONS OF THE MODEL

These proposals for organizational innovation—i.e., job circuits, council governance, colleges as life-cores

—involve several assumptions that can now be summarized.

One is that the university we seek—one characterized by "a new academic ethos of diversity and community"—"will require far more spontaneity in organization than educational institutions have commonly exhibited." [6]

Another is that the establishment of such an ethos would be encouraged by the innovations proposed here, because they emphasize flexibility, analysis, and change—necessary components of creativity—whereas the traditional bureaucratic form of organization is "characterized by high productive efficiency but low innovative capacity." [7] We should notice that the model for industry today is the decentralized, horizontal structure, emphasizing leadership that is situational and adaptable, with status determined not by position but by specific achievements.

Yet a third assumption, one focused on personnel more than on structure, hypothesizes the competency and goodwill of the participants involved in the work of the community. Selected faculty members are equal to the responsibilities of policy formulation

[6] Martin Meyerson, "The Ethos of the American College Student: Beyond the Protests," *Daedalus*, Summer, 1966, p. 739.

[7] Victor A. Thompson, "Bureaucracy and Innovation," *Administrative Science Quarterly*, June, 1965, p. 1.

in college offices, that function being distinguished from technical responsibilities which can be handled by trained functionaries. Students, for their part, at eighteen and older show as much maturity, poise, and social concern as the general adult population, and therefore may be expected to act responsibly when given responsibility. They, like faculty, administrators, and constituency representatives, have a contribution to make in community deliberations. This is, of course, a controversial point, one that is going to cause argument in academe during the next decade.

All of us have heard the principle arguments of those opposed to substantive student participation in academic policy formulation and institutional governance:

Students are immature and lacking in experiences appropriate to such responsibilities. Impressionable at best, at worst they are irresponsible.

Students have short-term connection with the school and correspondingly limited loyalty. They lack a sense of history or tradition and can bear no legal responsibility for the institution.

Students would be bored and impatient with what goes on at most faculty committee meetings and should thank God they are not obliged to attend. Furthermore, they have nothing positive to contribute to them.

Finally, if students can do a better job than faculty, they ought to be doing the teaching.[8]

Those of us favoring student participation view these arguments as hardly different or better than those used at the turn of the century to try to block the vote for women. Then, it was said, women were ill prepared for and disinclined to accept political responsibilities. Grievous consequences were predicted should the female suffrage movement succeed. It succeeded. Men survived. The nation prospered. It is better to develop mechanisms that take advantage of what students can contribute to effective governance than to be caught, to refer to another historical precedent, as were feudal lords yielding grudging acquiescence to the legitimate demands of serfs. But what, in fact, do students have to contribute?

The university is a center of learning and, consequently, what is heard in class is as important as what is said. No one is a better authority on what is heard than are students. Because we want to improve the educational experience and because we have no accepted way of evaluating the classroom effectiveness of professors, there is merit in structuring academic

---

[8] This is an abstract of responses selected from a stratified sample of full-time faculty members in nine colleges and universities who were asked, as part of a questionnaire on Institutional Distinctiveness and Student Development, Center for Research and Development in Higher Education, University of California, Berkeley, to indicate their ideas on student involvement in academic policy formulation. The full report is not ready for publication.

committees so that those who learn can work for change along with those who teach.

The university is also increasingly a center of computer-assisted learning, or of learning from teaching assistants, educational television, and so forth. Human and mechanical intermediaries are placed between the professor and the student. We need ways by which the students, those most affected by the new media, can report on how effective these teaching methods are. All we educators know for certain is that our experiences in an earlier day were not what theirs are now. Furthermore, as the first generation of the electronic age, students may be helpful in applying the insights of the new learning—with its emphasis on the convergence of men and ideas as opposed to the divergent tendencies of earlier epochs—to curriculum reform and other educational changes.

We ought also to remember that over 40 percent of the population of this nation is now under twenty-five years of age. Without resorting to claims of majority rule, inappropriate to the campus for a variety of reasons, students can properly emphasize that they are part of a large and important segment of society. In addition, when the economy is increasingly geared to youth and eager to rush them into consumer roles, when parents push them into vocational choices and social responsibilities, and the government hurries the young men into the military, it seems unlikely that colleges and universities can continue to represent the college years as a moratorium between childhood and adult life. When young people come to the campus they are young adults and should be treated accordingly.

Furthermore, it is contradictory to deny to students the right to critically examine and participate in the institutional aspects of the life of the university, their immediate world, at the same time that we are urging them to assert themselves in the even more complicated social and political institutions of the world beyond the campus.

Of course students have limited experience, a lack of legal obligation to the school, and a loyalty circumscribed by personal interests. But are faculty much different? It would be well to remember, before casting the first stone, how faculty success is measured by job mobility and how often it is said that faculty loyalty today is more to their professional guild than to their college. Students may identify with a college in a way faculty never will.

The frequent faculty comment that if students can do a better job in the classroom than can faculty then students ought to be teaching, is of course a caricature. Such an extreme reaction is not warranted. There is no evidence that more than a tiny minority of students want to take over the university, at the classroom level or elsewhere. Students in increasing numbers, however, are noticing that the academic community—which they had reason to believe was composed of faculty, administrators, and students—does not include them in governance. They see that in most schools, or at least in those places with the greatest influence, the "community" means faculty as the ruling class; administrators as second-class citizens, a necessary evil; and students as the tertiaries, a necessary anvil. But students have contributions to make to the issues related to governance, and the conviction grows that if students are required to be the anvil, they should also have a hand on the hammer.

Our commitments, I have said, are to an academic ethos of diversity and community; to innovations in governance that emphasize flexibility, analysis, and new leadership roles; to participation by faculty, administrators, and students in an organizational arrangement that not only tolerates but actually encourages confrontation within community.

Now, as a last statement on the rationale of this model, what Reinhold Niebuhr has argued for democracy, we argue for community: Man's capabilities make it possible; man's frailties make it necessary. The creative individual finds opportunities for leadership in community and the community provides correctives for his leadership. In community, interest groups prosper but their aspirations to power are checked. We cannot have educational institutions dominated by students, faculty, or administrators. Each segment has something unique and significant to contribute, and community makes possible the contribution of all.

Archbishop William Temple once complained that a university is "a place where a multitude of studies are conducted with no relation between them except those of simultaneity and juxtaposition." [9] Such a place, as accurate as the description is, should not be called a university. A true university has a sense of unity and is always concerned for the relationships of the one and the many, the particular and the general. This, after all, is what is sought by Chancellor Heyns, Archbishop Temple, and all responsible educators. This is the university as community.

There may be no such institutions now, but, under the influence of the integrative configurations required by our new world, such universities have an unexcelled opportunity to emerge; and the organizational arrangement most consistent with current potentialities seems to be one which views the university as an organic community emphasizing heuristic learning experiences.

[9] Quoted in Sir Walter Hamilton Moberly, *The Crisis in the University* (London: SCM Press, 1949), p. 31.

VI

A PHILOSOPHY
FOR THE QUEST

Throughout these chapters the appeal for diversity as a necessary first step to radical change in higher education has been balanced by a concern for values that finally will transcend the particulars of change. Computer technology is exposing the inadequacies of the space-time pattern of traditional thought forms and creating an environment featuring inclusive configurations antithetical to the atomization of the old industrial technology. Education for that future will need to be radically different from what it is today, and the testing of alternative educational models would be a start toward such change.

Yet the principal concern in all educational experimentation must be to give human contours to the developments of the nuclear-electronic epoch—to devise ideas, symbols, and values around which to cluster human experiences and make them truly integrative. Our commitment is to the whole man in a world culture; and no matter how diversified the philosophies of education or educational programs embodied in the various models, each will need to have certain internally unifying norms and values. Educators must show students that even in a world culture the whole man is one who can take a stand as well as show a capacity for change.

My contention has been that to date we have not shown this ability. Indeed, colleges and universities are a part of the problem rather than the answer. We are doing many things, but not the essential one:

Extending educational opportunity, requiring higher and and higher levels of faculty training, building buildings, raising money, adding new and more specialized programs —all these have their value, but none of them is a remedy for the deeper vacuity which comes from not having a coherent philosophy to tie the separate activities together and make them a rational whole.[1]

The solution will not come easily. There is no "coherent philosophy" in most institutions of higher learning because the society they are pledged to serve, and out of which their values have come, has no

[1] Manning M. Pattillo and Donald M. Mackenzie, *Eight Hundred Colleges Face the Future* (St. Louis: The Danforth Foundation, 1965), p. 31.

coherent philosophy. College and university presidents are wont to say that their institutions are "service oriented," meaning that they are responsive not only to the technical needs of the society but also to its social values. It is a position which has been stated by Hill and Dressel in this way: "Essentially the purposes of higher education are threefold: to preserve the cultural heritage, to pass on the cultural heritage, and to add to that heritage." [2] Such a definition gives insufficient emphasis to the role which higher education should play as social critic, and also fails to suggest that a university might best serve by standing apart from the culture, as a center of independent thinking. Furthermore, most administrators take their task to be the preservation and passing on of the cultural heritage, rather than the adding to it. But as values are flattened out in the culture and as philosophy in the society at large is attenuated, such a commitment becomes devoid of meaning.

THE VALUE VACUUM

Can the college and university be helped to meet the current vacuum in values by resorting to the authority of the church? The church traditionally has

[2] Paul Dressel *et. al., Evaluation in Higher Education* (Boston: Houghton Mifflin, 1961), p. 28.

claimed to be a conscience to society, and historically it has staked out the area of values as its domain. But the message of the church in modern times has been vitiated by the inability of churchmen to agree on the application of religious idealism to practical realities, or even to agree on the basis of religious authority itself. Certain of the contemporary theologians—Bonhoeffer (at least in his later writings), Bultmann, and Altizer and the "death of God" thinkers—have been eager to relate Christianity to modern man and to work out an accommodation with the secular world. As a result, what they offer has no distinguishable relationship to historical Christianity and hence sacrifices the authority of tradition. Such theologians seem determined to show that what is distinctive about Christianity is that it is not distinctive at all. For them the best Christian values are those which most nearly parallel secular values. Christianity becomes non-Christianity.[3]

Other modern theologians—Karl Barth (*Epistle to the Romans*), most Roman Catholic theologians, and the evangelical Protestant thinkers—conceive of everything as dependent upon God and his channels of grace: God must do for man what man is unable to do for himself. But although Christians thus possessed of the grace of God rationally might be ex-

[3] See Alasdair MacIntyre, "God and the Theologians," *Encounter*, September, 1963.

pected to be noticeably different and better men, there is no evidence that Christians of this persuasion have any advantage in the moral virtues. About them we can only conclude that the vessels have proved unfit for the blessing. This is the point, of course, that some believers make: that Christianity is not a matter of ethical standards, moral conduct, and measurable human accomplishments, but of something else— the acceptance of having been "chosen." The exterior life of the Christian, we are told, will be no different. What then is the difference, existentially, between this position and a commitment to an openly secular style of life? The Christian may answer that he works from a different motivation. But what difference does that make? Or it may be argued that to be a Christian gives one's life a different "symbolic significance." [4] But what difference does that make? What is the proof of the pudding? If it is not in the eating—then what?

These are some of the problems in looking to the church for leadership where we most need leadership these days if we are to break the anomie at the level of norms and values. We see one church faction gaining identity by removing itself from the arena of action and thus becoming irrelevant, while the other faction involves itself in the arena of action and thus

[4] Michael Novak, "The Christian and the Atheist," *Christianity and Crisis*, March 21, 1966.

139

achieves some relevance but at the price of an authentic identity. But both identity and relevance are needed to fill the vacuum, and these are not being supplied by the church.

Perhaps this is why students involved in the Free Speech Movement at the University of California, Berkeley—good students for the most part and with an active social concern—were markedly indifferent to organized religion. They were concerned about religious issues—the questions of the "ought"—but they felt themselves detached from the rites, dogmas, and traditions of the churches.[5]

Is it the nation-state to which college and university administrators should look for guidance when they pledge fidelity to the values of the society? Perhaps here is the source of the norms and values that can give dimension and substance to our lives. Theoretically, as I have said, the government is an agency of implementation for the will of the people, not an agent of innovation. Actually, the government has increasingly stepped into the value void and sought to become the initiator of change as well as the

[5] See the study by William Watts and David Whittaker, "Free Speech Advocates at Berkeley," *Journal of Applied Behavioral Science*, II (1966), 59: "It can be safely concluded that formalized religion, at that time, played a less important part in the lives of the FSM members than in the cross-section. It might be noted that this was a particularly stringent comparison since the atmosphere of the entire Berkeley campus would appear to be relativistic in religious orientation."

guarantor of stability. Yet because ours is a pluralistic society and a political state, the government may initiate only within the limits of an available consensus. This fact reduces the range of options, the choice of priorities, the style of the endeavor, and the assessment of consequences to the values acceptable to the lowest common public denominator. The effect is to level what the government can do to the point where meaningful distinctions are lost. John Lukacs, referring to Orwell's *1984* and denying that the future will bring totalitarian dictatorship, nevertheless fears that our future holds "a sense of impersonality together with a sense of powerlessness" that will bring on terrible consequences of another sort:

The danger for us is . . . the obverse [to totalitarian dictatorship]: the possibility of totalitarian democracy . . . a democratic society in which universal popular suffrage exists while freedom of speech, press and assembly are hardly more than theoretical possibilities for the individual, whose life and ideas, whose rights to privacy, to family autonomy and to durable possessions are regimented by government and rigidly molded by mass production and mass communications.[6]

Our society is in need of new goals to capture our loyalty by capturing our imagination. The drive for

[6] Lukacs, "It's Halfway to 1984," *New York Times Magazine*, January 2, 1966, p. 30.

wealth, power, and fame—those traditional American goals—no longer satisfy the majority of people. We have wrung the emotional satisfaction out of them and are jaded. As Kenneth Keniston has written in his book on alienated youth in American society:

Most Americans no longer want for material goods, adequate homes, or educations; starvation is virtually nonexistent; and our most pressing economic problems no longer concern how to produce enough, but rather how to distribute fairly the goods we already have and to live well and nobly with them. The abolition of poverty is within the reach of our society; and for most Americans, the achievement of abundance is a fact and not a distant dream.

With the age-old goal of universal prosperity within sight, we must question whether the methods—the technological values and virtues, the instrumental goals of our affluent society—that helped us approach this goal will serve to take us beyond it.[7]

The goals that we need for the future "beyond technology" are those that will encourage human fulfillment and beat back the ominous impersonality envisioned by Lukacs. These goals will be forged not by individuals dependent upon the status quo but by those with the courage to stand apart from it; not by

[7] Keniston, *The Uncommitted* (New York: Harcourt, Brace & World, 1965), pp. 427-28.

those who see only the possible in the realm of the present but by those with ideals for the future to which they make a wholehearted commitment.

If the conditions of modern times make it futile for colleges and universities to turn to the church or the government in search of norms and values, then they must turn again to the prospects within academe and ask that community to find the governing principles which will provide the normative elements for our educational programs. All administrators acknowledge, as Philip Selznick put it, that "the setting of institutional goals cannot be divorced from the enunciation of governing principles. Goal-setting, if it is to be institutionally meaningful, is framed in the language of character or identity, that is, it tells us what we should 'do' in order to become what we want to 'be' "[8]

Once again, the obstacles to the success of such an effort must be recognized. Faculty, on the whole, do not see it as their business to help set the general objectives of the institution in which they work, and their views, when stated, are so diverse or poorly thought out that their contribution is minimal.[9] Our responses have a way of revealing our priorities, and when faculty respond to questions of educational

[8] Selznick, *Leadership in Administration* (New York: Harper & Row, 1957), p. 144.
[9] See Dressel, *Evaluation in Higher Education.*

philosophy they usually show that their higher priorities are elsewhere.

If pressed to express themselves about institutional values, many faculty members declare a preference for a "rich diversity" from which the student will be free to choose and blend for himself. This approach has merit in proportion to the extent that faculty are willing to think out their contribution to that diversity and expose it to the assessments and correctives of their peers. But too often the harking to diversity is simply a ploy which, carefully used, frees the instructor from substantive involvement with students and permits him to take refuge in his own specialization. Yet it is impossible to separate knowledge and values, in either our personal or our professional lives; and faculty do in fact have something to say about general norms and values even while they profess to deal only with issues within their separate disciplines.

Knowing and valuing are in reality two facets of all learning processes, and one trouble with some college pedagogy is that it centers on the accumulative and ignores the affective aspects of learning. The teacher has to concern himself with how the student feels about what is offered to be learned.[10]

[10] Ordway Tead, *The Climate of Learning* (New York: Harper & Bros., 1958), p. 26.

Instructors with a concern for the student as a whole person must accept the responsibility for helping to lead the student to a reasoned framework of belief. "The student is no more likely to arrive at a sound world view effortlessly and by chance than he is to master calculus as a by-product of studying psychology or music." [11] Most faculties will have to change if they are to lead.

Although administrative officers are in positions of formal institutional leadership, they are even less likely than faculty to become involved in questions of purposes and goals. Most administrators exemplify Max Weber's classical theory of bureaucracy, with its emphasis on hierarchical authority and task specialization, and they try to refer all questions of policy to the "policy makers"—the board of trustees and the president. (Where, as we have seen, the matter of norms and values is floated out on the "public conscience" and never returns.) Most administrators are busy with means, not ends; realities, not ideals; particularities, not universals. The danger in this situation was perceived by Logan Wilson, President of the American Council on Education, who wrote:

Our real difficulty is that we lack the objective knowledge of causal relations needed to make well-informed decisions.

[11] Pattillo and Mackenzie, *Eight Hundred Colleges Face the Future*, p. 7.

. . . Administrative officers . . . are likely to be concerned either with quite specialized aspects of college and
university operation or with the *ad hoc* promotional problems of keeping the institution moving—and often without regard to where it may be headed.[12]

Administrators are also intimidated by fear of public
controversy. Values, they know, often create distinctions, and these in turn can lead to dissension and
social disintegration. This must be avoided at all
costs. Thus, those in administration are likely to make
conformity into a moral virtue because it aids control
and encourages stability.[13] Caught between the desire
for distinctiveness and the fear of differences, we
decide to err on the side of caution. Our operational
consensus on values becomes a collection of mean-
ingless platitudes which encourage conformity. We
gain unity at the price of diversity. We protect efficiency at the risk of integrity. The House of Intellect is comfortable but it lacks character.

While students have no inherent moral superiority,
their lack of public obligation and vested interest

[12] Wilson, "Myths and Realities of Institutional Independence,"
Fifth Annual Institute on College Self Study (University of California, Berkeley: Western Interstate Commission for Higher Education,
1963), p. 112.
[13] See Edgar Z. Friedenberg on this subject in *The Vanishing
Adolescent* (New York: Dell, 1963), pp. 92 ff.

allows them a certain candor in facing up to the condition of anomie. At least they talk of it openly. Yet they have been no more effective than faculty and administration in speaking creatively to the problem of institutional reform. They want education to be personal and relevant; they emphasize that the university must define its relationship with society and make clear its own hierarchy of values; they reflect wistfully on the need for "humanness" in educational relationships; but they are no more decisive about norms and values for complex structures than are their elders. In 1961 a study by Paul Heist showed that

most students have considerable difficulty speaking of their major values, let alone trying to describe how they may be or are changing. Questions regarding values frequently take them by surprise, and they have little to say, even after they have been holding forth quite eloquently on other matters. Repeatedly we are told that they have no real basis for knowing how much their values have changed.[14]

Since then the student concern for values seems to have heightened, but students, like the rest of us, are still without answers.

[14] Heist, "Student Values and the Academic Life," *Northwest College Personnel Association Newsletter*, Spring, 1961.

TOWARD RESPONSIBILITY

Our situation, then, is this: We are confronted by the absence of social norms and values which has resulted from the loss of traditional consolations and the paucity of leadership in contemporary institutions, including the church, nation-state, and school. We find that colleges and universities have been thrust by psychosocial changes into a position of responsibility for the establishment and refinement of values—a stance admittedly contrary to the historic role of public institutions but unmistakably a part of their present mandate. We can only conclude that institutions of higher learning must now move. They must find an answer for anomie. If models are no longer provided by other social institutions, and if, like it or not, education is the new religion of the young, then we have no honorable alternative but to take up the responsibility of leadership, not only in such areas as social graces, job training, and surface preparation for citizenship, but also in those having to do with philosophy and religion—objectives, values, and standards. Only so can we help to develop in students a capacity for good judgment. Only so can we secure institutional integrity, for "institutional integrity is characteristically vulnerable when values are tenuous and insecure." [15] Only so can we give direc-

[15] Selznick, *Leadership in Education*, p. 120.

tion to the expansion and change of the colleges and universities of tomorrow.[16]

For this formidable task the schools have certain assets: an aura of expectation in the public mind, based on faith and goodwill; growing financial resources and numerical strength; the best of society's intellectual, if not spiritual, resources; and a new sense of awareness, urgency, and determination in response to an evident need. We also have a reality factor—a certain "givenness"—that must be acknowledged. The academic atmosphere today is essentially secular, in most church-sponsored schools as well as in public education, and values are concentrated on man and his world. We are not responsive to authority that claims transhistoric and ultimate validity. Those who hold to divine revelation and the instruments of infallible authority—the Bible or church or whatever—are restrained by the fact that ours is a pluralistic society where, at least to date, the revelations, dogmas, and priorities of those claiming various forms

[16] The problem is not confined to this country. Stuart Maclure in Britain says: "The Robbins Report gave little guidance about what the aims and purposes of a modern university should be. . . . It is one of these academic ironies that it is only the latest, quite unprecedented, spate of new university foundation which has led to the beginning of any systematic study of higher education by the universities themselves—study which, in the nature of things, will be too late to help the present generation of pioneers." ("The University of Kent at Canterbury," *The Listener*, February 17, 1966.)

of absolutism have proved contradictory and unworkable. Thus, we must expect that the value judgments behind educational programs in the future will be those of mortal men working in a secular setting, whose efforts will be informed primarily by humanistic study.

Given the possibilities that challenge educators, the mandate that has been given them, and the realities of their time-space situation, what might be a viable approach for them, and for all concerned with education, to an answer for anomie? We need a way of getting at objectives. Colleges and universities will vary greatly in their statements of ends. What we must have is a broad conceptual framework within which all of us can meet and work at the task of defining our various objectives and modifying and improving those ends.

It has been my contention in these essays that a philosophy of education appropriate to contemporary developments and attendant needs will have two characteristics: It will begin by acknowledging the inevitability of value judgments, and it will end by emphasizing the provisional nature of all value judgments.

Concerning the first point, James Conant has written: "Literally, every step we take in life is determined by a series of interlocking concepts and conceptual schemes. Every goal we make, be it trivial or momentous, involves assumptions about the universe and about human beings." [17]

To live is to choose, and if not to choose, then to be chosen. We are "condemned to be heroic" in that we are required by the fact of life to face alternatives and make choices. Life does not proceed of itself. In some way, by certain values, we affirm life or deny it. We must begin here, and this gives us our foundation.

What are some of the value judgments we in fact have made that may be expected to inform the search for a reasoned framework of beliefs? Most of us, whether we acknowledge it or not, have taken a stance on the human condition in the social milieu. Educators affirm by their choice of vocation that man is a creature with a capacity for reason. We believe that man can learn, change, improve; the very structure of our institutions reveals that faith. But to reason, we also know from history, is not necessarily to be right. Nor indeed does it follow that to know the right is to do it. Man is possessed of psychological bias and influenced by social conditioning; he is determined by factors largely beyond his control, yet he possesses a measure of freedom and attendant responsibility; he is often insensitive, yet he has a unique ability for self-awareness, analysis, and criticism. While aspiring

[17] Conant, *Modern Science and Modern Man* (New York: Columbia University Press, 1952), p. 66.

to absolute certainty, he achieves only provisional certitudes.

The obligation to admit the tentative nature of all value judgments does not exempt us from the necessity of making them. Our commitments serve as the norms against which we evaluate attitudes and actions on a day-by-day basis, and they give value to our work through which a sense of community can emerge.

There is now a vast hiatus, I contend, between the "academic community" of our claims and the actual fragmentation and compartmentalization of working arrangements. Philosophical timidity, prompted by fear of controversy and a feeling of futility about issues which seemingly defy solution, has resulted in public colleges and universities being almost totally mimetic of what is thought to be the societal consensus on matters of values. At one time such an arrangement may have been tolerable as the best of bad alternatives. In other days the home and the church did provide criteria against which the public philosophy could be tested. But no longer. Now, whatever claims to "community" the colleges and universities may once have had, albeit from derived standards, have been lost through the demise of the former agents of authority. One effect has been the fragmentation of traditional social values in the schools according to the dictates of particular programs, departments, or dominant individuals. Another effect has been the vacuum created by the resultant absence of shared norms and values. Community is thus threatened by anarchy.

Earlier I mentioned certain of the presuppositions that figure in the value judgments we call certitudes. Now I declare others, for nothing is more dangerous than unrecognized preconceptions.[18]

If all certitudes of value are provisional because we are finite, then it follows that we are committed to pragmatism and relativism. Goals are instrumental and ethics contextual. We do not expect intellectuals to achieve a body of knowledge, first universally accepted as basic and certain and then communicated to students with the confidence of unity. Yet something more than the values of the mass media must fill the moral vacuum. The institutions of higher learning must now undertake what we may call the philosophy of the quest; it begins with the assertion of the inevitability of certitudes and follows with the acknowledgment that all certitudes are provisional. It always remains open-ended. But not empty. We see through a glass darkly, but we do see some things. We are subject to change, but we do take a stand. We try to extend the pragmatic goals beyond the immediate instrumental ends and we try to couple the ethic of individual honesty with an ethic of social responsibility.

[18] Moberly, *The Crisis in the University*, p. 62.

There are risks associated with the achievement of institutional character by pursuing an institutional rationale. The very success of the effort can lead to its downfall. Mechanisms erected to protect what has been gained can easily become barriers to criticism and obstructions to further change. The human tendency to absolutize achievements and assure their continuation by rules frequently transforms means into ends, a course described by Robert K. Merton as "the familiar process of displacement of goals whereby an instrumental value becomes a terminal value." [19] It is this problem which leads us to want sufficient flexibility for "constructive chaos" or "constructive imbalance." A certain ambiguity, fluidity, and alternation at the point of the "absolutes" may be the generator of change in a day when such change is needed.

The tentative nature of all value commitments has herein been posited as a defense against the premature solidification of gains. Our commitments are real and they are substantive, but they are not unchangeable. Recognition of this tenet encourages both criticism and creativity and assigns them fields within which to labor. And this is better than what now obtains in the realm of norms and values, where

[19] Merton, "Bureaucratic Structure and Personality," *Complex Organization*, A. Etzioni, ed. (New York: Holt, Rinehart & Winston, 1961), pp. 53 ff.

nothing can be determined and therefore nothing attacked.

My attempt in this essay, in summary, is to move toward a philosophy of education that can provide an answer for anomie without substituting rigidity for vacuity. It is an attempt to apply the concept of change to that philosophy without robbing it of content and continuity. It is a philosophy that begins in the human condition, acknowledging the complexity of human nature and the diversity of human experience. It faces the necessity of making value judgments on issues that are as complex as the human agent who must make the judgments.

In a secular world characterized by relativism, in which man is required by the exigencies of human experience to act and react, we have available a philosophy that is substantive though not sacred. Within the provisions of this philosophy we can develop purposes, goals, procedures, and arrangements that will provide for our colleges both institutional character and individual distinctiveness. We can give guidance to administrators in the delineation and evaluation of their work; a contextual framework within which faculty have freedom for their responsibilities; as well as norms and standards against which students can test themselves and by which they can establish their own answers for anomie. We can also provide, at the same time and under the terms of the same philosophy, encouragement for the creation of alternative educational models that will be bridges, not only to the past but also to the future.

This is one strategy for reform in higher education and one that gives hope for an alternative to irrelevance.

INDEX